THANK GOD
for the
Cotton

THANK GOD
for the
Cotton

Memoir of a Mill Worker's Daughter

Sybil D. Smith, PhD, RN

AMBASSADOR INTERNATIONAL
GREENVILLE, SOUTH CAROLINA & BELFAST, NORTHERN IRELAND

www.ambassador-international.com

Thank God for the Cotton

ISBN: 978-1-62020-511-2
eISBN: 978-1-62020-416-0

This is a work of nonfiction. Some names and characteristics of the individuals involved have been changed. Any resemblance to persons living or dead is coincidental and unintentional.

Cover Design and Page Layout by Hannah Nichols
eBook Conversion by Anna Riebe Raats

Printed in the USA

AMBASSADOR INTERNATIONAL
Emerald House
411 University Ridge, Suite B14
Greenville, SC 29601, USA
www.ambassador-international.com

AMBASSADOR BOOKS
The Mount
2 Woodstock Link
Belfast, BT6 8DD, Northern Ireland, UK
www.ambassadormedia.co.uk

The colophon is a trademark of Ambassador

I dedicate this literary work and aging recollection of events to
my family
of the past, present, and future.

CONTENTS

PREFACE

I WAS BLESSED WITH WHAT my mother was denied, a family unit. The Baptist church became my mother's surrogate family unit. The church at the Connie Maxwell Baptist Orphanage extended the goodness of God across Mom's early years as her wounds unfolded. When my family of origin unit, the post orphanage generation, was challenged with events that could not be understood, it was our community of faith that came near, extending the love of God. It was the deep well of God's goodness that brought the healing of generational baggage.

In the past two years, I have buried both of my parents who had been married to each other for over seventy years. Adversity comes across our lives, but it is how we handle the adversity that matters. God does provide the way for us to overcome difficulty. God has His big picture plans and provisions for us, as well as day-to-day decision opportunities for His goodness to be bestowed. This memoir is an example of God's grace as provided one day at a time. Faith, hope, and trust lived out in simple lives in simple ways can crescendo unlimited goodness. The great aha moment does come. Devastating events can transform into good as God provides the way out of the unexplainable.

ACKNOWLEDGMENTS

A GRATEFUL ACKNOWLEDGMENT IS MADE to my husband. This work is brought to bear by his support and encouragement. He was insistent this story be told. In our fifty-four years together, Mike has always been the stabilizing force. He was anchored in a strong and open family network. Before entering the military, he had lived his entire life in the same community and attended the same church. Solid Christian values guide his life. He takes responsibility for his actions and knows when to speak, and when to keep silent. His strengths compliment my weaknesses. Further acknowledgment is extended to his larger family, my in-laws, as they extended the goodness of God to me in many loving ways.

Cotton was a means used by God to anchor my life in His life-giving ways. My paternal grandparents came from the backwoods of the North Georgia and North Carolina mountains. In the days of prohibition, the bootlegging of liquor was the means of income. Many of the mountain folk were sent to federal prisons for running moonshine. The owners of the cotton mills recruited labor from the mountains. The cotton mills offered a regular job and village housing. The recruiters offered a cleaner and safer way to live. The mill villages had churches where God's truth was made available. God's provision of the cotton at my intersection in history was His care for this child. I thank God for grandparents who heeded the call and left the mountains for a better way of life in the cotton mills.

INTRODUCTION

HOLY WEEK 2017

MAUNDY THURSDAY

As it was my usual morning practice, I intentionally took time to gaze out of the back side of our home. It was my special time to thank God for another day, and for sharing His creation with me. From the back windows and from our deck, I could see the skies above the wooded area. The wooded area was about a hundred and fifty feet from the back of our home. As I would daily raise my arms to the skies in gratitude, I was now able to thank God in advance for whatever the day would hold for me. I had always admired the view from our back yard, however, for many of those years I had only a shallow understanding of my relationship with its source.

The feeling in the air was without flaw. The humidity, the barometric pressure, and the sound of the birds were a blessing to experience. I walked out across the yard to the edge of the woods for further examination of the dogwood trees. They were in full, exquisite bloom today. Our weather cycle had made this Holy Week very special with the dogwood trees. We did not always enjoy the blessing of the full bloom of the dogwood trees every Holy Week. My Dad had planted the dogwood trees for us over forty years ago. I broke off a bloom and recounted the Easter legend in the dogwood bloom.

As I turned to walk back toward the house, I was met with a sugar maple tree that was also planted forty years ago by my Dad. Unlike the dogwoods in full bloom, the maple tree was early in its journey to its fullness for the season. The tree was about halfway between the house and the woods. This was a miracle tree. Many times, over the years, the tree had been struck by lightning with large patches of bark stripped off, split, or had limbs blown off in heavy storms. However, every Spring the tree would surprise us as it put out new growth. Some of the blackened scars on the bark persist to this day. My husband never did want it cut down, and in later years he started referring to the tree as the Shane tree. Shane is the name of our son, and he also is a survivor of many lightning strikes and hard winds blowing across his life.

When I got back up to the house, I rested my arms across the railing of the wheelchair ramp coming out of the deck door. I was able to look up into a different direction and I became captured by the silence of the blue sky that surrounded me. It was a glowing sky, blue with not one cloud present as far as I could see. I gazed down onto the boards of the lower elevation of the wheelchair ramp. With my eyes, I followed each plank of the ramp all the way up to the entrance of the deck. The silence of the sky was singing alleluias. Along with the alleluias, the words of Reginal Heber's hymn, "Holy, Holy, Holy," were coming forth from the entrance to the deck.

God had used that ramp to bring healing to this child in ways never imagined. The ramp had been used to culminate a twenty-three-year journey of spiritual healing on first thought. However, in

reality it culminated the promises of God over the lifetime of someone wanting to do right, thinking she was doing right, but missing
the mark.

The ramp was constructed nearly two years ago when my homebound father came to live with us. He was with us a little over four
months before joining our Heavenly Father. We were so blessed to
have him with us. He enjoyed going up and down the ramp and getting out onto the drive way in his wheel chair. Of course, he was
unable to propel the chair, but on pretty days he enjoyed our pushing
the chair out near the end of the drive and watching the cars go by.
He would always wave at everyone. He enjoyed watching the activities that took place in the field across from our home, the animals
and the gardening. Some of the kids in the neighborhood were generous in spirit and would come by the house and sing with him. We
referred to it as the Jesus Loves Me Choir. On one occasion, he told
the choir that he knew Jesus loved them, but that Jesus also loved
him. From that time on, the song became Jesus Loves Ed, using his
name and, not the word, me.

When we go to church tonight for the communion service, we
will be asked to reflect on the Last Supper of Christ with His disciples. In my solidarity with Christ, I will also be having communion
with my earthly Dad. We were blessed to have communion with Dad
about an hour before he went to our heavenly home. The hospice
chaplain came by at just the right time. I gave Dad a sip of water after
the chaplain left, kissed his forehead and told him I was sitting right
beside the bed. His breathing just stopped about thirty minutes later.
There was no noisy struggle for air. I was so blessed to be right beside
him as he began the awaited journey to his eternal home.

Throughout Maundy Thursday afternoon, my mind was flooded with all of the memories from childhood, and all that had brought me to this point in my life. I had good memories along with inner celebrations of the grace and mercy God has made available to me. I discovered meaning and purpose in my life and living during a season of suffering. Being able to care for my Dad was a continuation of my healing, a time of rejoicing in the goodness of God. As we remember the Last Supper tonight most likely, based on previous experience, little will be mentioned about Jesus washing the feet of the disciples.

It was about twenty years ago when I attended a workshop at a Christian university about spiritual healing. The nuance was created from the outset with a song I had never heard before, "The Basin and the Towel" by Michael Card. For me, the song put practical application to finding meaning and purpose in daily living (See appendix A).

How blessed I am this Holy Week. I can get outside and admire the gifts in nature. I am getting old, but my body parts are working. I am not confined to the inside of a building. I have friends and family. It is with deep gratitude I will seize the solemn reflection opportunities this Maundy Thursday.

GOOD FRIDAY

The service last night provided contemplative wanderings in my mind with the power of silence allowing me to travel to an abiding joy within. I looked around and saw friends who were caught up in grief and sorrow. I remembered the times I had sat there just like them.

I went out to my deck looking over the trees to another cloudless sky. The gratitude I felt was overpowering. Could it be for real?

From where things had been twenty plus years ago it seemed like a dream. Why should I be so amazed? Our God is in the prayer answering business.

Our son and grandchildren would be coming up in the afternoon to attend a special Easter production in Greenville as we had been doing for several years. The production usually goes into vivid detail about the suffering of Christ. This year we were taking the young girl next door with us to the drama. She was one who would come and sing with my Dad. She turns twelve tomorrow and when I think about it I am amazed that she was only ten years old when she would come and sing with my Dad in his closing days on this earth.

We all made it to the Rodeheaver Auditorium. Even though the program did cover the resurrection of Christ, I was left with an awareness that on Good Friday our Savior was placed in the tomb. Following the drama, we enjoyed a good meal together. We sang Happy Birthday to our young guest over a birthday donut. I cannot speak for the others but my mind would wander to the words of the hymn, "Low in the Grave He Lay."

EASTER EVE

This morning, I was out at first light. It is hard to believe we have had three beautiful days in a row and tomorrow is expected to be the same. Once again, I raise my arms in gratitude and give special thanks to God Almighty that I can stand here and gaze at His beauty. I think about those who are in nursing homes and can no longer get outside, and some without a window to even see outside. Do you think nursing home residents who are alert may feel they are in a situation in which they have no control or input? Can they live with hope in their limited environment? There are many around us who struggle every day with the bleakness of limited options. There are many unheard cries on the church pew every Sunday.

On Easter Eve we remember that Christ was in the tomb this day so that we do not have to live in the tomb. We remember this was the day He did battle for us. Hopelessness can feel like a tomb. My husband and I do volunteer work with hospice patients and we hear all kinds of stories from the patients as well as the family members, some with hope but more with fear and uncertainty. As we reflect on Easter Eve, will we be dithering with egg hunts, church music, and meal preparations?

Or should we be looking for some solitude where we can contemplate exactly what our role is to those who are entombed and living all around us? As the old hymn by Clara Scott goes, do we need to ask God to, "Open my eyes that I might see?" However, if we ourselves are entombed with our own baggage, we will not be able to see those who are buried alive all around us.

When Christ washed the feet of His disciples at the Last Supper, did that not instruct us to look around for those who may need a foot washing? Some folk may choose a lifestyle that results in entombment. Some may be in various stages of the journey trying to get out of a bad place. Others may be kept in the tomb by those around them. After all, just as Jesus had the Pharisees wanting to keep Him in the tomb, we still have Pharisee types today that want to keep others entombed.

RESURRECTION DAY

There is no mistaking that our sunrise today tells us that Christ is alive. His tomb is empty. He lives today just as He said He would.

My job is to carry His resurrection power to others. There is hope for those who live with feelings of hopelessness. They do not have to stay in the tomb. I need the solitude in my life that brings enough silence for me to hear the hushed sobs and tears. I need to be equipped with the basin and the towel at all times.

I was fifty-three years old when I had a foot washing and began my journey up out of the tomb. In the depths of my brokenness, God surrounded me with an army of support for the journey. The healing path was set before me. It took years, little by little, to find the healing as provided for me each day. When I could accept each day as it came to me, I was at peace. That was the beginning of my morning prayers of thanksgiving. I learned to trust the boundaries God was going to provide for me this day. After all, today is what I have. The goodness I receive this day is to be shared with all.

In looking back over the years and the agonizing growth process, I learned to thank God for things of the past. His goodness was always there in ways I could not see back then. One thing I learned in later life was to thank God for the cotton. The cotton industry made a way for my family. For me, the journey started in 1945 in Greenwood, South Carolina. In the closing year of my Dad's life, we had the opportunity to rekindle the unity of community we once knew on the mill village where my Dad was raised. Life and living on the mill village back then was held together by the village church. God provided a way for us to experience that unity together once again with old and new friends. The mill villages were not free-standing municipalities. The villages consisted of houses located on mill-owned property that surrounded the mill itself.

How blessed I am this Resurrection Day! Hallelujah: Presente.

CHAPTER ONE

LAUREL ROAD

MY FIRST CLEAR MEMORY IS around age four when we lived at what is known today as 577 Laurel Avenue E, Greenwood, South Carolina. Back then it was called Laurel Road. We moved to Laurel Road from what I can vaguely remember as an apartment on the side of another person's home. It was located on a road going out of town past the former Carr Biscuit Company, where my father, Edward Columbus Tipton, was employed as a shipping clerk. His first job when he got out of the Army was working for the phone company in Greenwood. He got the job with the phone company because he had been a communications lineman in the Army. As a paratrooper in Europe, they jumped in behind enemy lines and set up communications before the ground troops arrived.

From that apartment, we moved to the four-room house on Laurel Road and we also had a car at that time. Owning a home and a car was a rare thing back then. My Dad was raised on Greenwood Mill Village (current location is 475 Draper Avenue, Greenwood, South Carolina) and his parents, Ma (Wessie Lee Allen Tipton, 1891-1957) and Pa (Levi Webster Tipton, 1881-1958), still lived there. Greenwood Mill was a cotton mill where bales of ginned cotton were processed into cotton fabric. Dad was named after one of Ma's brothers, Columbus. I fondly remember the visits to Ma and Pa' s home. The mill village houses were all painted white and were very close together. You could live in a mill house as long as you worked in the mill.

We would always enter the back door of the village house. Immediately on the right when entering was a four-foot-wide bench with a high back that had a framed mirror attached. The mirror was eye level for a standing adult but a child had to stand on the seat of the bench to see in the mirror. There was a leather strap hanging on the left side of the mirror. Pa shaved with a straight razor every morning. A basin of water was placed on the bench and he would sharpen his razor on the leather strap. He would stand in front of the mirror and shave.

On the left side of the room was the kitchen table. The wood cook stove was directly ahead of the entrance door, and there was a wide opening into a room on the right of the stove. The cook stove had burners of sorts on a waist-high surface, and up above the burners was a two-door shelf. Ma always had biscuits and real meat up there. The round burner surface could be lifted up with a lever and wood placed in under the burner. There was an oven under the cooking surface. No matter what time of day we arrived, the warm biscuits and real meat was there for us. Real meat was what I came to know later as fried fatback. The aroma had a satisfying scent.

Going to the right out of the kitchen into the middle room takes you to an area with quilting frames suspended from the ceiling. A bed was over in the immediate right corner. Ma and the neighbor ladies were always making quilts in that room. Over to the far right of that room was a door leading to a little hallway that had an in-door bathroom with a tub on legs and a toilet. There was no heat in the bathroom and the toilet paper was very stiff. Sometimes we used pieces of newspaper for hygiene. The other side of the little hall opened into two rooms where my Aunt Ruth and Uncle Jack lived and shared the bath. My cousin Lonnie lived there also. When standing in the kitchen door and looking straight across the middle room, you could see the front room that doubled as a sitting room and extra bedroom. Pa had a mantel Seth Thomas clock that sounded every hour in the front room. The middle room was the only room with a heater. Of course, the wood stove kept the kitchen warm.

Spit cans were in all rooms since most of the family members and friends dipped snuff. Snuff was a ground up tobacco product. The dry powdery substance was placed beneath the lower lip and it cre-ated heavy black spittle that frequently had to be expelled. My mother pronounced snuff as a very nasty habit, and that no one in our house could ever dip snuff. The talk was that in the mill there was nowhere for folk to spit so they spit their snuff between the looms.

Often when we visited with Ma and Pa we would go out to the shed behind the house where Dad had carrier pigeons. They roosted on the beams in the ceiling area. We would feed and water them. Dad would occasionally send one out on a trip to a friend's place nearby. The pigeon would return. Carrier pigeons were part of the commu-nications he learned to set up when in Europe during World War II.

Westside Baptist Church was located on Greenwood Mill Village and we would drive from Laurel Road to church on Sundays before going to Ma's for lunch. Often I would spend weekdays at Ma and Pa's home. Around four o'clock in the afternoons, Ma would let me walk down the sidewalk beside the house and I would see Pa walking up the sidewalk coming home from the mill. He would always have a piece of peppermint candy for me. Sometimes he would also be carrying eggs.

Back at our Laurel Road house, we had an oil heater in the front room that kept things fairly warm. We had a telephone with a four-digit number - 7417. We also had a refrigerator whereas our neighbor had an icebox. An ice truck would bring them a big block of ice each day to keep things cold. We had a bathroom with a four-legged tub and a toilet. There was no sink and no mirror. We had to use the kitchen sink. Dad nailed a small mirror over the sink so he could see to shave. Later when Ma and Pa moved into the Laurel Road house, Pa moved his shaving bench with mirror from the kitchen on Draper Street into the bathroom on Laurel Road.

Mom and Dad both smoked Lucky Strike cigarettes. Dad was open about his smoking but Mom did not want anyone to know she smoked. She always went into the bathroom to smoke. If you ever saw her smoking, she got angry. She smoked but preached against snuff. There were many conversations over the process of quitting. By the time I was in the third grade, they finally did stop smoking.

On weekends, some of Dad's friends would come over and play football in the side yard. One day, Mom started yelling for me to get the guys up to the kitchen. There was a large snake in the kitchen sink. They came and carried it out the back door and killed it. I had a brother who was two years younger than I. Strange as it may seem, I do not have much memory of him while at Laurel Road.

I remember being left by myself sometimes during the day when my mother would go off. I am not sure where my brother was. Most of the time, I would stand and look out the front window until she came home. If the weather was nice I occasionally went to a neighbor's house.

My Dad built swings for us in the garage door entrance-way with ropes holding the swings up to the top of the door frame. There was a slot on each side of the doorway and we were to keep the wooden seat of the swing in the slot when we were not swinging so not to block entrance to the garage. Pa was over one Saturday and noticed the ropes were fraying on the door frame because of use. He proceeded to cut the swings down because he felt the rope would break on us. My brother and I both were upset with Pa. Daddy acted like he had nothing to do with it.

Sometimes my brother and I would wander into the wooded area at the back of the property. There was a big gully back there where trash was dumped and there was some minor debris scattered throughout the area. Often, we would explore curious looking items and on a few occasions, we found a bundle of money. We were so excited to find money and would run up to the house to tell Mom or Dad. Every time, we were told to just throw it away because it was confederate money and had no value. The neighbor lady told us the same thing also. No one wanted to keep it.

In the first house down below us was a lady who did not go to church and did not work in the mills. My Mom did not like her and complained about her, but she did keep her yard neat. Below her was the Thompson family and they had twins. Sometimes I would go down there when my Mom went off. Mrs. Thompson let me play out in the yard. I did not go inside.

In the house up above us was a girl I played with some. They acted like they were better than us. I never understood that. Across the road and up from us was a two-story white building and Mr. Leary had a store downstairs. We did not buy much from Mr. Leary. We bought most of our groceries at the Tolbert's Grocery on Greenwood Mill Village. Mom would call in an order and Tolbert's would deliver the groceries to our home. I would go in with my Dad frequently when he went in to pay our bill.

We often made trips over to the Greenwood Mills ball park. My father was a passionate baseball fan and former textile league player. One time I remember the car would not crank and we walked over to the ball park at Greenwood Mill Village. Right before being drafted into the Army during World War II, Dad had a conversation with the Cincinnati Reds as it was called back then. An offer was made but the draft prevailed. When he returned from the war, the Cincinnati scouts approached my Dad a second time but he had no interest. He had injured his back in Germany and had some limitations. However, it was something we could never talk about. He did not want anyone to know he had an injury. Dad feared that if folk found out he had a back injury it would keep him from getting a job. He kept it that way until the day he died even though he would have been eligible for benefits. He was satisfied in helping others become baseball players. Dad's story was confirmed after he passed away in 2015 when a former mill hill friend and textile baseball player told us the same story about Cincinnati trying to recruit Dad on two occasions.

In early 1951, a buzz started up about the new mill village being constructed where all of the houses would be brick. The new mill under construction was called the Harris Plant, and it would run synthetics and no cotton. The Harris Plant and village was owned by the same man who owned the Greenwood Mill and village.

At the same time of the Harris buzz, our family had a special buzz of its own. That was the same year that Pa would no longer be able to work in the mill because of his age of seventy. A family could only live on the village as long as they were working in the mill. Since my father was working as the shipping clerk for another company, he applied for the shipping clerk job at the new Harris Plant. With Dad going to work at the Harris Plant, we were eligible for a mill house on the Harris Mill village. The decision was made that we would move to the Harris Mill village when the houses were ready and my grandparents, Ma and Pa, would move into our home on Laurel Road. Also on the Harris Mill village was a new elementary school which would open in time for me to start the first grade fall of 1951.

CHAPTER TWO

HARRIS MILL VILLAGE
– LANETT STREET

THE HARRIS MILL VILLAGE WAS comprised of well-built brick homes, a school, and a shopping center. The Harris Community was the last mill village planned and constructed by management for company employees in the United States.[1]

In the summer of 1951, we moved into 100 Lanett Street on the Harris Mill Village. Since my Dad worked in the office, we qualified for a six-room house with central heat. We did not have air conditioning, and did not get a window fan until I was in the sixth grade. The four and five room houses had only fireplaces and most of the folk did buy an oil heater and backed it up to a fireplace to vent. There were a few seven room houses on the village for the "big bosses." The houses rented for one dollar per room per week. So, my Dad had six dollars per week deducted from his pay. Payday was Thursday for the plant workers, and the office workers got paid on Fridays.

---

1 *International Directory of Company Histories*, Vol. 14. St. James Press, 1996. Pp. 210-221.

Behind the houses was an alleyway on each block. Each house had a fifty-five-gallon trash can in the alleyway and all trash was picked up by a mill truck each week. Residents in mill village housing under the umbrella of Greenwood Mills also received free laundry. Special large draw string bags were given to each home. All dirty clothes were to be placed in the labeled bag and placed on the porch for pick up every Tuesday morning. By midday every Wednesday, the clothes bag was delivered back to the front porch with the washed and wet clothes in them. Every home had a four strand clothes-line in the back yard. We had to buy our own clothes pins. I would reach into the bag and pull out the garments and hand them to my Mom to pin to the lines. Every back yard had laundry blowing in the air on Wednesdays. Later I became tall enough to hang them all by myself. I never did complain about this chore because it was nice to have clean clothes. We also had milk delivered to the house in glass bottles three times a week but it was not free. The milkman would collect every Friday.

My Dad told me that "old man Self" who owned the Greenwood Mills would often walk, from his mansion style home, across the golf course and through the mill village to his office at the Greenwood Mill. Supposedly, Mr. Self was moved with emotion one day seeing so many women out with wash pots, boiling the water, and wringing the clothes. From that emerged a centralized laundry department at the mill and thus, all of Mr. Self's mill villages started receiving laundry pick-up and delivery to the door front. While telling me that story Dad also told me about how he had a part-time job as a caddy at the golf course and that was where he learned to play golf. Later, he went on and got a part-time job at the State Theater in downtown selling popcorn.

The Harris Village Shopping Center which was located on Center Street consisted of: a gas filling station, café, barber shop, beauty shop, branch bank, US Post Office, and a grocery store with a pharmacy. The groceries were considered a little expensive. Across the railroad track from the mill was a one room grocery store where you could buy single items, and you could charge items if you had no money. I would go up there all the time for my Mom, picking up one item at a time just to get supper on the table. My mom made very good biscuits and gravy which would go with just about anything to make a meal. On Fridays, I would walk with my Dad up to Langley's store to pay the bill and Dad would always let me pick out a penny piece of candy.

CHURCH LIFE

There was no church at the Harris Mill Village when we arrived. Often we would drive back to Westside Baptist Church on the Greenwood Mill Village and attend Sunday School and preaching. Preacher Byars was the pastor. In Sunday School each week, the teacher, Miss Jennings, would place a sugar cookie with a hole in the middle on our little finger at the close of class.

After the Harris Village began to populate, the folk wanted to have church meetings on the village. Harris Mill officials made two empty houses available for church meetings, one for Baptist and one for Methodist. Westside Baptist Church worked with Mr. John Styron, a lay minister, who was employed in the mill and lived on the village to start Baptist church meetings. As the group grew, we were allowed to meet in the gym of the Harris Elementary School. My Mom was a charter member of the new church start. Dad was not, even though he attended regularly.

Years later, I learned that the owners of the cotton mills across the South always wanted to get the churches started. Supposedly, they expected the churches to keep undesired activities of the mill workers in check. The preachers were expected to preach against drinking and other unacceptable behaviors.

Sometime after the church was chartered, some men from the church came over to the house and spoke with Dad about accepting Christ as his Savior. I remember seeing him kneel in prayer with the men. A few weeks later he was baptized outside in Little River on the other side of Greenwood. Years later, my Dad told me that he had accepted Christ on the battlefield in Germany during World War II but never did make a profession of faith until we were living at Harris. Our church life became the center of all we did while living at Harris and the rest of our days.

I came to know the Lord during a revival meeting while the Harris Baptist Church was still meeting in the schoolhouse. The folk who accepted Christ during the revival were baptized at the Westside Baptist Church in the baptismal pool.

The church life set the being of our family. Our lives revolved around the church, Harris Baptist Church, from the start-up meetings in houses, to meeting in the school gym, to building and moving into our own physical church building. The mill gave a block of land for the new church building. The ground-breaking service, and even down to picking out the colors for the walls, was daily conversation.

There was one very memorable Sunday evening worship time before we got into the new building. Our community went into a sudden high alert because a hurricane was heading our way. We all packed into a center room of the meeting house and stayed in there long enough to all become miserable. Finally, the men decided the worst had passed over and we were out of danger. It was a little scary walking home.

Before moving into our own actual church building, my parents were involved in leading various groups within the congregation. One summer, my Dad accepted responsibility for the director of a new start-up program, Baptist Training Union, BTU. He went to the association meetings in town to find how it was to be launched and operated.

Soon after school was out that summer, Dad started announcing IPTA plans in all church meetings. It went on every week, IPTA, IPTA, IPTA. Everybody planned on coming in September. He never revealed what the letters, IPTA, meant. Interest grew and grew, and the talk was taking over the village. Curiosity seekers overflowed the September meeting room since the village wanted to know what IPTA was. Dad thanked everyone for coming and then announced that our church was launching the Baptist Training Union. Everybody still wanted to know what IPTA was. When he could delay the crowd no longer, Dad revealed IPTA: "It Pays To Advertise." Then he explained, without such build up and expectation, how else would so many attend the launching of BTU. BTU turned into a very meaningful program and called the village together into age segregated fellowship every Sunday evening. Sunday mornings were filled with Sunday School and preaching. On Wednesdays, we met for prayer meeting, choir practice, and children programs, Sunbeams, Girls in Action (GAs) and Royal Ambassadors (RAs).

On Sunday mornings, my Dad would drive about a mile out of the village and pick up an elderly lady, originally from Panama, for church. She was always thrilled about attending and desired for her daughter and son-in-law, with whom she resided, to attend. On rare occasions, her family would come to church. She had a grandson in my grade at school. On weekday evenings after supper, my Dad and one of his friends, Mr. Bud or Mr. Styron, would walk the village and call on folk who had not been at church the previous Sunday.

I can remember only one Sunday School teacher from Harris Baptist Church, Mrs. Dow. There was one verse we had to memorize and repeat every Sunday morning, Psalm 19:14, "Let the words of my mouth, and the meditation of my heart, be acceptable in thy sight, O Lord, my strength, and my redeemer." It became a part of my being that continues even today. I continue to pray it on a daily basis. Mrs. Dow always kept us in check. The person that led my sister's group was not as successful in maintaining her pupils because my sister started biting classmates when they nicknamed her and did not call her by her given name in Sunday School.

The books of the Bible were memorized by the young people as we had sword drill competitions. A sword drill is when you have to rapidly look up Bible verses. Knowing the books of the Bible was essential for success.

Week long revival meetings were held every Fall and Spring. Many folk attended the meetings and many came to know the Lord. The music was very memorable. I just do not hear those revival hymns much anymore. Some favorite lines include: "By and By When the Morning Comes," "Looking for a City," "When the Roll is Called Up Yonder," "Love Lifted Me," and "Amazing Grace" was always a fervent one. Today we refer to it as old-time gospel music. For us, it was all we knew. Until our church building was completed, the baptisms were held at Westside Baptist Church at Greenwood Mill Village. There was a lady named Shelby Jean who lived off the village and she became our music director. A lady named Lucile Roberts who lived on the village played the piano.

Vacation Bible School was held every summer. We would go for five mornings of Bible stories, fun, and games. We had special refreshments of Kool-Aid and cookies. The Kool-Aid was made in large wash buckets which contained a block of ice. The buckets were about two feet in diameter, a foot deep, and made from a galvanized steel. We could get extra drink but not extra cookies. Different folk took turns going to the ice plant picking up the blocks of ice.

HOLIDAYS ON THE MILL VILLAGE

Holidays were special on the village. About the only time we got any fruit was near Christmas when a truck from the mill would deliver large fruit baskets to every house. It contained apples, oranges, grapefruit, a bag of mixed nuts in the shell, and a box of candy canes. It was rare to have fruit at any other time of the year.

At Christmas, my Mom and Dad took effort to see that we always had a tree with lights on it, and we always got a surprise gift. We received a thick Sears, Roebuck and Company catalog about a month before Christmas. My brother and I were always looking over the pages for something we wanted Santa to bring us. About the middle of December, Dad would start reading "Twas the Night Before Christmas" to us at bedtime. Dad was always singing Christmas songs to and with us, especially "Here Comes Santa Claus." There was much suspense in trying to sleep on Christmas Eve since Santa would be showing up during the night.

One Christmas was a challenge for me. All of my friends were asking Santa for a bride doll. Every time I brought it up, I was told no. One day, my Mom showed me a picture in the catalog of a naked doll that did not cost much. Then she showed me a picture of doll clothes that could be purchased. So, Santa brought me a doll with a wedding dress on it but it did not look like the dolls that my friends received. It was embarrassing as folk made fun of my doll. I guess I knew for sure that year that Santa was fantasy talk. My Mom did make some other clothes for my doll so mine did have more than one outfit.

My mother's sisters would always send us a gift for Christmas. One year, Aunt Margaret from Georgia sent me a Kodak camera. Wow, what a treat. Of course, it took money to buy the film and to get the photos developed. Eventually, I got a paper route and had some spending money. Then there was the Christmas my brother and I got bicycles from Santa. We put miles on those bikes. My Dad liked riding them also. We had baskets on our bikes and when my sister was about two years old, Dad would put her in the basket and ride her around the block. Another very memorable Christmas morning was the year we got cowboy and cowgirl outfits, and the boots.

Until my Mom was in her sixties, we always had two very distinct aromas in the home over the holiday season between Thanksgiving and Christmas. First was the smell of fruit cake in the oven. The ingredients in the fruit cake were expensive and had to be purchased in town. The second great aroma was Mom's caramel candy. She made it by dumping white sugar in a cast iron frying pan. As it heated, it liquefied into a thick brown syrup. At just the right time, heavy milk was added to stiffen the syrup to the consistency of oatmeal. Then it was dropped a teaspoonful at a time onto wax paper and set up until it cooled down. Neighbors were always wanting her to make a batch for them. Sometime they would bring us a bag of pecans in trade.

Easter was a very special time. For weeks before Easter, everybody in the church was involved in preparing the Easter music and drama play. Everyone would be talking about what they would wear on Easter. It was like a festival of fabric, patterns, and sewing machines. Ma had a Singer treadle sewing machine that came to our home when they moved out to Laurel Road. I still have the machine. Ma's feet had begun to swell and she no longer sewed. Neither did she have quilting frames out on Laurel Road. However, we were well supplied with her quilts that kept us for years, even into my marriage. The Easter Parade was something my Dad started singing about several weeks ahead of Easter. It was a tune from a movie watched while he sold popcorn in the theater. The song was about your Easter bonnet with all the frills upon it. On Easter morning, we all strutted the two-block walk to the church while Dad sang.

The Fourth of July was a big event because the mill shut down for the week. Many went on vacation. We never had money for big vacations like some took for the entire week. But one year we went down to the zoo at Grant Park in Atlanta for a day trip. Another time we went to Stone Mountain near Atlanta. Stone Mountain has the largest high relief sculpture in the world. The Confederate Memorial Carving depicts three Confederate heroes of the Civil War, President Jefferson Davis, and Generals Robert E. Lee and Thomas J. "Stonewall" Jackson. The entire carved surface measures three-acres, larger than a football field and Mount Rushmore. Can you imagine a sight like that back then and the enormous impression it had on poor mill hill kids? The history is recorded on the Stone Mountain Park website.[2]

We would also visit my mother's sisters who lived in Atlanta. Another time there was a day trip to the Candler, North Carolina, area where Ma's family originated. We went to Aunt Monte's house where I saw my first spring house. There was no refrigeration inside the home, but outside they had built a little shed over a spring in the creek. Items were kept in the cold water for storage. One year we went for a two-day trip to Rock City, Lookout Mountain, and Ruby Falls, near Chattanooga, Tennessee. Ruby Falls was located in very deep caverns and was a gigantic waterfall. We also had village traditions for April Fool's Day, May Pole Dance, Halloween, and Thanksgiving.

Much excitement filled the village approaching Election Days. I did not fully understand it back then as I do now. There was always much whispering in front of the kids about things. The Cold War was raging and everyone was fearful of Communist spies being near. In the schools, we had bomb drills. Sirens would go off and we would hide under our desk. Anytime an airplane flew over (which was not often), you were relieved that you did not get bombed.

The Cold War issues were open conversation that the kids could hear. In both 1952 and 1956, most adults felt relieved that Eisenhower was elected even though the village folk were expected to vote differently. The whispers we were not supposed to hear were about folk that were not allowed to vote, and what if they showed up at the pole. We did have a police deputy on the village and it was feared he may not be able to handle the situation.

---

2 http://www.stonemountainpark.com/Activities/History-Nature.

The voting place was on the covered walkway area that was between the gas filling station and the café in the village shopping center. There were two booths of sorts made of two by four wooden frames covered in a loose fitting fabric. If the wind was strong the fabric blew loose.

OUR FRIENDS

My closest friends were mostly those who attended the Harris Baptist Church with us. There was one boy on our block who attended the Methodist church and he was okay. All but one set of siblings lived on the village. Closest to me were the two girls who lived across the street from me, and they were the ones I spent many nights with when Ma was living with us. They had an older brother who had a job at the drive-in theater a few miles away and to get to and from work, he drove a motor scooter. Occasionally we would get a ride with him around the block on the back of his scooter. On such an occasion, we were traveling fast and I was holding on for my life. All of a sudden, I had a big shock on my buttocks and started screaming and yelling. He stopped because a spark plug had shorted out or something like that. I saw him fifty years later at a reunion and he would still laugh and tell that story. My motor scooter driving friend had become a wealthy man. When the mill sold off the village houses, the residents no longer had trash pick-up. The opportunity was seized and a major trash collection service was developed. In 2015, the trash collection service celebrated fifty years of being a family owned business and serving the Greenwood area.

There was a wooded area behind the row of houses on Hutson Street and many of us played in that wooded area. We would rake back the pine straw from a large area, and then we would take a stick and scratch out a house plan in the dirt and mound up pine straw piles and make rows for the floor plan with the straw. With our pretend house we would play out different roles of housekeeping. It was our playhouse until the next rain or wind storm when we would build another. We also pioneered out a few trails in those woods. One went up to the paved highway, now called Calhoun Street. Across the road was a railroad track that ran down both sides of the village and on into the town of Greenwood. Up the road to the left was where we had to cross the tracks to get over to Mr. Langley's store. Center Street was the name of the street that ran in front of the Village Shopping Center and on over to cross the railroad tracks to Langley's store. At the store, it turned into a dirt road and ran on down past the store.

A few families had a television. I enjoyed visiting around and getting to watch television with them. We finally got one around 1955. I enjoyed watching: I Love Lucy; Father Knows Best; Amos and Andy; and Roy Rogers to name a few. My Dad liked to watch sports. Before we got our television, my Dad would go up to Mr. Hill's house and watch Friday night boxing. Sometimes I would go up there with him and sit on the porch or play in the yard. I could hear the television and often they spoke about Gillette Cavalcade of Sports.

Our backdoor neighbors were the Thomas family. They moved to Harris Village from Shelby, North Carolina. Mr. Bud Thomas had worked at the cotton mill in Shelby. They had two girls and a boy. The two girls went to work in the mill. The oldest of them got married to a man who worked in the mill and they got their own house on the village. The son was the one who organized and kept our backer-sac games going. We used to take kitchen chairs from inside our house and sit in a circle in the joint back yard and talk away the afternoons. Sometimes on the weekend, one family would go into town and buy a bag of ice while the other mixed up the recipe for ice cream. The Thomas family had an ice cream churn. It was a special treat on those hot summer days to have ice cream. We also enjoyed watermelon together in the backyard.

Another rule of living on the village was there were to be no vegetable gardens. Mr. Bud found a way to plant a few tomato plants each year that could not be seen from the street. He always shared with us. Tomato sandwiches were a big, good thing.

A sadness came over our neighborhood one day when Mr. Bud came home from work with the diagnosis of tuberculosis. The health department had been doing screening at the mill. Mr. Bud was rushed to the tuberculosis sanitarium in Columbia and stayed for nearly a year. Since his daughter who lived in the house worked in the mill, they did not have to move off the village. In the meantime, the health department made sure no one else had tuberculosis. Mr. Bud's wife was frail and did not get out as much as most folk. The church and village ministered appropriately.

While Mr. Bud was in the tuberculosis sanitarium, his daughter hired a black lady, Florence, to come help with the cleaning and cooking. Having help in the home was not uncommon back then but most folk could not afford help. Mr. Bud's wife was weak and there was no one to take up the slack with him gone. Florence had to walk down a long dirt road to get to the village. It enraged my Mom that no one would go pick up Florence or take her home. If our car was at home when Florence would get off work in the afternoons, Mom would watch for Florence to start walking up the street. Mom would drive going the opposite direction around the block and pick up Florence when she got on the next street.

Sometimes I would ride with my Mom. It was down the long red clay dirt road, beside Mr. Langley's store, with tall trees and thick, heavy, vegetation all around. We would turn left into a long drive way to a dilapidated house and Florence always expressed much thanks when she got out. Mom fussed all the way back home about how our neighbor should not treat Florence that way. At Christmas, we carried food to Florence and her family.

On a few other occasions, Dad would take my brother and I down that same road a short distance to a creek. We would seine for minnows with a net we made from a meshed vegetable sack. Our second and final seining adventure ended when a large water moccasin snake appeared out of the heavily bushed area, poised to strike my father's leg. We raced out of the creek screaming. We talked about our fright for years.

On the surface, life seemed good at Harris. However, undercurrents ran deep in our home. I did not comprehend it all at the time. Things happened that I did not understand. I did not hear my friends talking about things like what went on in my home. I could not understand why my Mom was so well liked when she did some of the things she did. I knew it was not right but I did not know how, or was afraid to ask questions. At times, it took great effort to just go day to day. I held on to what my Dad frequently told me, "Work hard in school and you can go to college and have a better life."

My mother lived with unresolved abandonment issues her entire life. I was a college graduate before I was able to begin to put the pieces of the puzzle together.

CHAPTER THREE

BACK ON LAUREL ROAD WITH MA AND PA

AFTER MOVING TO HARRIS VILLAGE, we went back on a regular basis to visit Ma and Pa who were in our former home on Laurel Road. Sometimes my brother and I would spend the night with them. Pa's mantel clock would chime on the hour all night long and kept me awake. We always had heavy cover under several of Ma's quilts. The food was good. Ma still had her wood burning cook stove. We would play in the yard and visit the neighbors. I always wanted to check out the trees my Dad had planted when we lived there. There was a row of what we called cedar trees planted on the lower border of the property. I later learned they were Leyland cypress. Then there was my favorite among the existing trees, the chinaberry tree. The chinaberry tree made some shade in the front yard and we could sit under it on hot days. There was always vigorous discussion about the stinky berries that came out in the summer. There was strict instruction to never try to taste a chinaberry.

Ma would always make us brush our teeth even though we did not have toothbrushes. We would go into the yard and stand around a spirea bush. Ma would break off a branch and remove the foliage. She would break the branch into three to four inch lengths. She instructed us to start rotating the end on our teeth. As the stick got moist, the end turned fibrous and we thus had a toothbrush. We had to clean each of our teeth with the spirea brush. I do not recall when I got a real toothbrush but sometime in my early school years, my Dad carried me into town to a dentist, Dr. Fuller. I had many cavities and Dr. Fuller pulled the teeth with no deadening. It was a painful experience that lingered in my memory for years. Sometime after that I did have a real tooth brush. Most of the time we could not afford toothpaste but Dad taught us how to brush with baking soda. It was after I was married before I ever went to a dentist again.

Pa stayed busy tending the yard. He would walk into town sometimes. Pa was faithful to wind the mantel clock with a special key and made it a distinctive event for us as we watched. Pa was a steady person. My father was one of four children. My father was as steady as his father was. However, his siblings struggled for years before their lives stabilized. It seems my Dad, the youngest child, and his father had to frequently put out the fires in the lives of the siblings.

My three cousins on my father's side came up in broken homes. I think part of Pa's steadiness came from his background in the mountains. In the mountains, they did what they had to do to earn a living for support of the family. Sometimes supporting the family meant making and running moonshine. Moonshine was illegal liquor, and it brought profits during the prohibition years, 1920-1933. They also grew the corn for the moonshine production. Much had to be overcome in the North Georgia mountains where Pa was born.

There was a day when Pa came to realize that staying in North Georgia had nowhere good to go. Pa never told that story to anyone in Greenwood, but I learned about it years later when I visited Big Creek Church community in Fannin County. At that time there was one cousin left and I heard his version of why Pa left Fannin County. Pa left Fannin County, Georgia, with a team of mules and ended up in Buncombe County, North Carolina, working in the logging trade. It was in Buncombe County where he met Ma, Wessie Lee Allen, whom he later married. They lived on Old Candler Town Road, Candler, North Carolina.

When the cotton mills started recruiting labor from the mountains Pa went to Pelzer Mill in Pelzer, South Carolina, with the promise of a house with running water and an indoor bathroom. From Pelzer Mill, they moved to Greenwood Mill in 1927 for better pay and a bigger house.

My oldest cousin Lindsey, Aunt Ruby's son, did graduate from high school and went to Clemson as a football player. The family was so proud of Lindsey. It was a very sad day when Lindsey showed up on our doorstep at Harris and told us he had to drop out of school to get married. He married Joyce and we came to love her and their children. She came from a stable home and that helped balance things out for many years. However, there came a season of reckless living. There was a divorce, remarriage, divorce and remarriage to Joyce. Lindsey died before Joyce. Joyce and their kids helped take care of Lindsey in his later days.

Ruby, the mother of Lindsey, had a second marriage to a man from Cuba called Johnny. Johnny had four children. They all came up from Florida and stayed with Ma and Pa for about a month. They spoke a strange language. While they were there we did not go over to Laurel Road as much. They returned to Miami. In Ruby's later years, she was widowed in Virginia by her third husband who did leave her some money. My Dad became her responsible party by default.

My Aunt Ruth and Uncle Jack, who had shared the Greenwood Mill house with Ma and Pa, had to move out when Pa left his Greenwood Mill job. Aunt Ruth and Uncle Jack worked in another mill in town owned by a different company. They moved down the road a piece from our Laurel Road house. They were first in a place with no inside plumbing. It was not long before they found another place nearby and it had inside plumbing. Jack had a problem with alcohol and had a hard time holding a job, but he managed to hold on to a mule and about an acre of land to farm. Aunt Ruth worked the night shift at a cotton mill in town. There was a constant chatter about her need for gas money. They also raised two hogs for slaughter each year and had a smoke house where the meat was cured. They had one son Lonnie, who was a year younger than me.

When we would go back to visit Ma and Pa, we always went on out to see Aunt Ruth. Their place was close to the Greenwood Airport and because of all of the bomb drills in school, I would become very frightened every time a plane came over. There was an un-grassed area near the house that seemed to be hollowed out except for the rock formations. It was occupied with large rock formations like you would see in the Western cowboy movies. My brother, our cousin Lonnie, and later Dicky, and I would play Cowboy and Indian out there until we got called to the house. In the backyard of the house, Aunt Ruth frequently had a wringer washing machine set up. The clothes were washed first and wrung out. The soapy water was drained from the machine and refilled with a hose. They were rinsed in the clean water and wrung out a second time and then hung on the line. It was hard work to have clean clothes after leaving the mill village.

Dad's older brother, Fred had a problem with alcohol also but he always maintained a job. When he was sober, he always sang in a church quartet and helped with church music. Of course, he was frequently changing churches and jobs. When he was married to his first wife, Rosa Lee, he worked at Harris Plant and lived on the village near us. When you lived on the mill village and you lost time on the job because of the drinking, you also lost your house along with your job. Rosa Lee left Fred after a drinking episode. She also left behind their son, Dicky, who was a year younger than me. Fred was forced out of his mill house and brought Dicky to our home and asked my Mom to keep him for a while. That set up much turmoil for my Mom. She was angry. We carried Dicky over to stay with Ma and Pa for a few days.

Mom went to Laurel Road to pick up Dicky and got back to our house about the same time Dad got home from the plant. Mom had found out where Dicky's Mom, Rosa Lee, was staying in Abbeville with her sister. My brother, Dicky, and I were loaded into the back seat. Mom was forcing Dad to make the trip. We drove to where Rosa Lee was staying. Mom carried Dicky to the door and informed Rosa Lee she would not be raising her son. Rosa Lee did not want him. They argued and Dicky started crying and screaming as he chased the car, "Don't leave me," over and over. At that time, I did not know what I was witnessing but I too cried most of the way back to Harris. Mom spent the next week defending her actions. Dad was very quiet about it all.

For years after that event, I remember my Mom bragging about how she handled the "nerve of that Rosa Lee walking off and leaving

Dicky behind." She felt wronged by Fred bringing Dicky to our home thinking she would take care of him. Inconsistency seemed to be the way of life for my Mom. Church folk only saw a kind, gentle person who helped others, but there was another side of her. I could tell that Pa was wise to her ways.

Rosa Lee relocated to her home town in Social Circle, Georgia. My Dad, brother, and I did go down there some and visit Dicky. One time, Pa went with us. Mom never went. Dicky stayed in Social Circle for about two years. Fred brought him back to Greenwood and he lived with Aunt Ruth for two years. He and Lonnie became close. With Dicky out there it gave us a foursome to play Cowboy and Indian reenactments together on the huge rock formations.

Pa had a brother, Wylie, in Louisville, Kentucky. Pa rode the bus to go see him and also to go to the Kentucky Derby while there. Aunt Ruth came over to stay with Ma while Pa was gone. Pa became ill while in Louisville and had to have his appendix removed. He could not ride the bus back home. My Dad and cousin Lindsey drove up to Louisville and brought Pa back. It was not too long before Pa was back to his usual self, coming and going. I am not sure if my Dad was exposed to horses while in Louisville but he did develop a keen interest in horses.

Ma's health began to change. On most every visit to Laurel Road, we would find Ma's ankles to be more and more swollen. Over time it became hard for her to move about. In 1956, when she could no longer get out of bed, we moved Ma into our house on Lanett Street. The church helped us locate a sick bed for her. Pa would stay some nights with us and sometimes go back to Laurel Road and stay.

CHAPTER FOUR

SCHOOL DAYS

I STARTED FIRST GRADE AT Harris Elementary School shortly after moving into the house on Lanett Street. There was one class for each grade level. The school was located at 103 Eastman Street which was 0.6 mile from our house. We walked it every day. It was referred to as the other side of the village. Sidewalks were available but we often walked through a wooded area, which made the trip even longer but was much more fun. Children who lived near the village also attended the village school. A bus would pick them up and carry them home. I went through the sixth grade at Harris Elementary. By the time I got to the seventh grade, a junior high school had opened several miles from the village and we were bused to the new Northside Junior High School.

The first grade was an exciting time. I could go somewhere everyday just like my Dad did. My teachers took a special interest in me so I felt special. Years later I came to realize it was because of problems they recognized in the home. My teacher, Mrs. Sheally, was strict about teaching the ABCs and the numbers. Writing or printing upper and lower-case letters was done every day as well as for homework. If you did not quit talking when told to be quiet, Mrs. Sheally would slap the back of your hand with a ruler. If you were a repeat offender, you would have to go stand in the coat closet. It was not easy for the family to provide paper and pencil. If you ran out before payday, someone may loan you a sheet of paper but you had to pay it back. Usually you could round up a nub of a pencil somewhere. At home, if your pencil needed sharpening it had to be sharpened by Mom or Dad with the kitchen knife. At school, there was a pencil sharpener on the wall beside the chalk board and the lines were long at the pencil sharpener every morning. If you could afford a number three lead pencil, the point did not break as often, but most everybody had number two pencils. There were monthly assembly meetings, consisting of all of eight grades. The assembly meetings were for announcements, and at each assembly meeting one grade would put on a skit or sing for the group.

A music teacher would come to the school on Thursday each week and teach singing to each grade level. We would march single file down to the music room which had a piano. At the end of the school year, a singing program by combined grades was presented to the parents in the evening.

At the school house, we had a cafeteria which was a new thing in those days. For twenty cents per day you could get a hot meal. Lunch money was collected once per week. If you could not pay the one dollar per week, you had to bring a lunch from home. I always had lunch money but I do remember a few kids not getting to go through the lunch line. They sat in a different place in the cafeteria and somehow always seemed to get something to eat. Peanut butter was always mixed with honey and a big bowl of the sweet prize sat in the middle of the tables of eight. We would verbally fight over the peanut butter. I always heard the peanut butter was a military excess and sent to the schools. I do not recall anything unpleasant about the plates of food given to us. It was just a good thing to get the food.

When school was out in the summer, the Methodist church group on the village held a day camp of sorts for the children. We would gather for games, and playing in the school play yard on swings, see-saws, and a monkey bar. Jumping rope was a big thing. Two people would hold a long heavy rope and turn it very fast. You had to run in and start jumping. If you missed the rhythm and hit the rope it would burn your skin. If it was raining, we would go across the street to the Methodist church meeting place. On Thursday of each week, the recreation center from town would send a bus to the village, pick us up, and take us into town to the swimming pool.

Ever so often there would be competitions at the pool. Several times I won the longest distance in the underwater swim. Our prize for winning was free tickets to get in to the pool on other days. My Dad would always take us when we had the free admission tickets. I always hated getting into the showers after a swim but understood the need to wash off the chlorine.

Another thing which took place in the summer was the book mobile visits to the village every week. The book mobile always parked in the side lot of Langley Store. The lady who operated the book mobile placed me on a special reading path each summer. I always completed the plan she made for me. One series I read was *Susannah*, about life in the old southern plantation days. The story was about the best friend of a white plantation owner's child. The friend was a black slave child on the plantation named Susannah.

Susannah was always teaching life lessons to the plantation own-er's child. I was also a recipient of Savannah's life lessons. Between the first and second grade, I had my tonsils removed at the old Greenwood Hospital. It seemed painful for a few weeks but I under-stood it was to protect me from getting sore throats in the future.

My second grade teacher was Mrs. Dendy. My sister was born in October of the second grade. When I was in the second grade, my cousin Dicky entered the first grade. In the third grade, I had Mrs. Cobb for a teacher. My brother entered first grade that year. We now needed two dollars per week for lunch money. I did go and talk with Mrs. Sheally about my brother and ask her to let me know if he needed any help. She was gracious. Between second and third grade, I went to Camp Rawls Sunbeam Camp for a week. I remember it as being mostly church stuff, playing games, swimming, and singing.

I worked hard on all of my assignments and received good grades. However, there was one thing I started noticing. With all of my teach-ers, there was a trip with my Dad to their home in the evening or on a Saturday. I was aware that none of the other students ever talked about visiting the teacher at their home. None of the teachers lived on the village so there had to be some reason we went into town for such a visit.

When I got to the fourth grade my teacher, Mrs. Hartzog, fre-quently invited my Dad and I to her house. Sometimes Mrs. Hartzog would pick me up on a weekend day and carry me with her on a day trip to visit one of her married children. I thought it was strange that I never heard of her taking any other students on trips. I do not recall that I was ever told not to talk about it, but there was something that made me aware that it was not happening to other students.

Between the fourth and fifth grades, I went to Camp Long 4-H Camp. There were fun and games at this camp but it was more about learning to sew, cooking, washing clothes, and keeping clean. They taught us how to make shampoo and toothpaste from things around the house. During the school year, health department nurses would come to the school and talk with us about hygiene and brushing our teeth.

After receiving so much special attention from my grades one thru four teachers, I was aware that my fifth-grade teacher, Mrs. McKenzie, had no interest in me. I worked hard and made good grades. There were no visits to her home with my father after school hours. In the fifth grade, we had to memorize all of the states and the capital city for each state. The test was oral with us standing by a blank map of the United States, while Mrs. McKenzie pointed to each state and we had to name it and the capital city. Hawaii and Alaska were not yet states. I do recall being very embarrassed on several occasions that year when I had no socks to wear to school. I had to wear my brother's boy socks. Some students laughed at me. Even Mrs. McKenzie would stare at my feet.

It was during the fifth grade that we had a special student enter our class. He lived off the village and rode the bus. Jimmy was crippled from polio and had to wear a special boot and brace on his leg. Jimmy was likable and sometimes would come to the church on the village. I did become curious about polio and wanted to know more about it. We had just started having to take the polio vaccine at school around the same time. There were many stories about the "iron lung."

We also had a cripple girl that was starting school about the same time. She had a birth defect with one leg shorter than the other and had to wear a shoe with a three-inch lift on the sole. She eventually went to Shriners Children's Hospital in Greenville and had surgery to correct her problems. I learned later that her condition was called scoliosis.

By the time I entered the sixth grade, my grandmother was sick and came to live with us. Much of the time Pa would stay over at night. There was much turmoil in the house with all of the sleeping rearrangements and the extra load of care my Mom had to accept. I performed well in class.

Mrs. Teddards always had some special projects for me to work on. She privately worked with me helping me to learn the metric system. I was the only student studying the metric system. At one point, I was explaining the metric system to other students and collapsed to the floor. They put some wet paper towels on my head and I regained consciousness and just sat down for the rest of the day. I collapsed like that one other time when in church. I just fell to the floor. When I came to, I sat down for a bit and got ok. My Dad and I also made one of those awkward trips to Mrs. Teddards' home one evening for some unknown reason to me.

In those days, the loud speaker system in the school could deliver both good and bad news. No one wanted to hear their name called out telling you to come to the office. It was never for anything good. Yes, there was the day that the speaker came on with the usual, "Attention, may I have your attention." The message continued, "Diane Tipton, please report to the principal's office." Everybody sighed and stared me down. I was terrified.

I walked down the long hall and as I leaned to make the right turn to travel the next hall, the janitor, James, was standing in the doorway of the janitor's storage room, which was jokingly called his office. James was a kind, gentle black man and we all liked James. He was always helping us. James was looking at me in a weird way. He had heard the announcement also.

When I got to the principal's office, I was told to sit down in front of Mr. Schuller's desk. He came in and very sternly took his place behind the desk, opened his desk drawer, and pulled out a bullet. As he rolled the bullet around, he queried me about whether I knew anything about the bullet. As he showed me the end where the hammer of a gun would strike, he told me that site could be hit by something when it was not even in a gun. If so, then the bullet would go off, explode, and possibly injure someone. I assured him I knew nothing about the bullet. Then I learned my brother had brought the bullet to school that day. I was instructed to tell my Dad about it and have my Dad come to the school the next day.

I do not recall much about the rest of that day. I hurried home, told my Mom and told my Dad when he got home at five. I do not remember that my brother received any punishment or reprimand to the degree the ordeal of being called to the office had frightened me.

In the Spring of my sixth grade, Ma passed away in our home. Shortly after Ma died, my Mom informed me she had gotten me a job delivering papers. Greenwood had an afternoon newspaper Monday through Saturday. I was horrified about being a girl and delivering papers. I had seen only boys doing it in the past. My route was the part of the village where we lived.

On Fridays, I had to knock on every door and collect thirty cents for the weekly rate. If I did not find a customer at home on Friday, I would have to go back and collect on Saturday morning. Usually it was pretty easy to collect the entire route over a weekend. Occasionally I would try to catch somebody at home during the week.

The newspaper office had set up a special arrangement at the branch bank in the village shopping center. When the Friday papers were brought to the village, they would include a bill for me. It would be the amount of money that I had to take to the bank and give to them for the payment on the newspapers. Anything collected over the amount of the bill was considered my earnings for the week. It was usually around two to three dollars.

It was good to have some money. One of the first things I bought for myself was a raincoat and some rubber galoshes to keep my feet dry. Of course I had to save up for several weeks to have that much money. Most of the kids had these items and were able to stay fairly dry on rainy days. It was just something we could not afford and I spent many days cold because I was so wet from walking in the rain to school. Also, the raincoat and galoshes made delivering the paper a lot easier on rainy days. It was years later in the eighth grade before I got my first umbrella.

After seeing me with a paper route, my friends, Betsy and June, across the street from us, got the paper route for the other side of the village. We three girl paper carriers set the example for women libbers back then. Their father, Henry Bell, ran the gas filling station at the village shopping center. The newspaper bundles for my side of the village and their side of the village were dropped off at Henry Bell's gas filling station.

We would come home from school, usually get a snack and something to drink, and then walked down to the gas filling station. I would load my newspapers in a canvas sack that fit around my neck. Betsy and June would envelope-fold all of their newspapers into a little box shape, ready for slinging on the porches before loading their sack. Then they would start out walking to the other side of the village to their paper route. On my route, I just folded the next paper as I slung the one for the previous house and I got the job done as I went.

Sometimes my brother would help me with the paper route but he had some problems that made him unavailable at times. He had a fireworks accident on the Fourth of July. He lit a cherry bomb in his hand intending to throw it off the porch. It exploded in his hand as he pulled his hand up by his ear for pitching it off the porch. There were the burns to get over but lingering for years was the injury to his eardrum. Local doctors could do only so much. My brother had to start going to Greenville to see the ear specialist for treatments.

About two years later he had surgery on the eardrum. He was also born with a contracture of the left foot that required a special doctor and shoes that required trips to Greenville. There were certain foot manipulations that had to be done on his feet each night that became a ritual. His foot eventually straightened out, like the other one.

By mid-summer every year, the village talk was all about getting ready for school. We had to start thinking about our clothes, shoes, paper and pencils for school. Going barefoot in the summer was the way it was. There were the briars, splinters, cuts and scrapes on a daily basis. We got two pair of shoes a year. There were the lace-up oxfords when school started each year, and then for Easter we usually got a lighter pair of shoes. When we would go into town, we would spend hours walking through the stores and seeing all the choices for clothes and shoes. Usually we had identified what we wanted before having the money to purchase.

After I got my paper route, I was excited to have my own money to go buy the kind of shoes I wanted for school. I was tired of the usual saddle oxfords and I had noticed that the JC Penney store in town did have some solid tan colored oxfords. When I had finally saved up the money, my Mom drove me into town and let me out. With three one-dollar bills and some change in my hand I went in and showed the man what I wanted to try on. I sat down in the chair expecting him to get his foot measuring device. He looked at my feet and told me he could not let me try on shoes because my feet were too dirty. I showed him my money and he shook his head no. It was a deep wound to my inner being that lasted for years. I got up sobbing silently as I left the shoe department. I walked around in the store staring at merchandise until my eyes dried. Finally, I got it together enough to go out and wait on my Mom to pick me up. I just told her they did not have my size.

Over the next few days my mind went into problem-solving mode. While I had been walking around in the store, after being denied, I had noticed a table with pairs of plastic looking ballerina shoes rolled up and selling for one dollar. My plan became that I would go back the next Saturday to get the ballerina shoes for one dollar. Then I would wait until the next trip into town. Ahead of time I would wash my feet thoroughly, dry them completely, and wear the ballerina shoes into town. I knew I would have to walk very easily because the shoes were so thin. I did not want the plastic to tear and my feet get dirty before I got there.

The plan worked. The shoe salesman was willing to measure my feet and try the shoes on my feet. The purchase was completed and I had tan oxfords for the seventh grade. The wound inflicted by the shoe salesman was not dealt with until I was fifty years old. Shame can be bottomless at any age.

By the time I entered the seventh grade, we had moved to Beacon Street. This was the first year the seventh and eighth grades were moved away from the Harris Elementary School. We rode the school bus to the new Northside Junior High School. There was no one else from Harris in the class with me. We changed rooms to a different teacher several times a day and sometimes I would see friends from Harris in the hall. One thing I learned quickly was that you wore a stigma if you came from a mill village. Then when they found out I had a paper route, the stigma grew.

In the seventh grade, I had the opportunity to join the band. You could rent an instrument for four dollars per month and the lessons were free. If you played the percussion section, you did not have to pay rent. Therefore, my decision to play percussion was easy. It was enjoyable and I learned to play the snare drum, cymbals, and bass drum. It was a lot of fun and I met people who did not discriminate so much. We were all learning to make music together.

I got to know a few people that did not live on a mill village. I asked my Dad if I could invite a classmate over one afternoon, and then if he could drive her back into town when he got home from work. He agreed. I extended the invitation. She asked her parents and they agreed. I had failed to inform my friend about the paper route and that she would have to accompany me on my paper route when we got home. She was shocked, to say the least, when we went up to the gas filling station to get the papers. As we walked the route, she got interested in folding the papers and throwing them onto the porches. By the time we finished delivering the papers, Dad was home and we drove my friend to her home in town. She remained my friend but never did invite me to her home.

It was during the seventh grade that Pa passed away unexpectedly. I was surprised that my seventh-grade teacher visited our home a day or so after the funeral. Again, my Mom felt imposed upon by Pa's relatives coming in and out. She had no tolerance for anyone that cried. She was constantly fussing about Dad's sister, Ruby.

At the end of the seventh grade, I gave up my paper route.

In the eighth grade, the girls had to take home-economics while the boys all took wood shop. We learned to cook and sew. I had already been sewing some but not to make a garment to wear from scratch. Ma's sewing machine had been with us ever since they had moved to Laurel Road. It was in this class that I learned to follow a pattern and how to finish off a garment with buttons and do the hem stitching. It empowered me somewhat to have some control over what I wore. But I still had to find the money to buy the fabric, thread, a pattern, and buttons. Sometimes I would take buttons off an old garment and reuse them.

I made friends with Jane who lived on a farm. She sat in front of me in several classes and we talked of many things. One day, she asked me about some bruises I had showing on my arms. I told her I had some worse than what she was looking at and I would show her in the bathroom. On the next break we went to bathroom. I raised my skirt up exposing my thigh with cuts and bruising. It was shocking to her to think I got spankings that left those kind of marks. She was an only child and rarely got spanked.

Then almost every Friday, I was invited to go home and spend the night with Jane. Her family owned acres of pasture land and we would walk the pastures as Jane explained to me about how the farm was operated. We could walk for long distances and never lose sight of their house. We never discussed the issue about the markings on my body again but the family gave me respite on a regular basis.

Sometime during the eighth grade, I was called to the office and became very uncomfortable when they talked with me about running for vice president of the student body. I would be running against someone who was the son of a medical doctor in town. I was instructed to go home and ask my parents. They agreed. Even though I knew about it in advance, I was mesmerized when the announcement came over the intercom that I was running for vice-president of the student body.

I did not know what to do next but my mother sure did. She organized all the village kids in the church that attended the junior high, taught them songs to sing, made posters and much excitement was created in the school election process. Nonetheless, I lost to the doctor's son. I never did understand my Mom's involvement unless it was to support the underdog, and she did have big hearted emotional responses to underdogs over the years.

At the close of every school year, my Mom would have me write a letter to Sybil Foster. I had been named after Sybil Foster who had been a social worker at Connie Maxwell Orphanage and had much positive influence on my Mom's life. Miss Foster had helped my Mom get a job after high school. My assignment was to let Miss Foster know how well I had done in school because she may send me a present. Most of the time I did get a Christmas present from her.

CHAPTER FIVE

MA'S DYING AND DEATH

WHEN THE DECISION WAS MADE to bring Ma to our home, a sick bed for her was placed in our middle room. Diapers had to be made from sheets and pieces of cloth. They had to be hand washed on a regular basis. There seemed to always be an odor. A double bed was also in the sick room. A cot sort of bed was added to one of the other bedrooms since Pa would stay over sometimes.

Most folk with a six-room house who had to create a sick room used the front room beside the kitchen. My Mom insisted on having a formal looking dining room that was rarely used. She got a used mahogany table from a former Draper Street neighbor of Ma and Pa. The project to refinish the table went on and on. There was major drama until she obtained the six, most perfect, new store-bought, mahogany chairs. The chairs stayed with us long after the table was gone. Mom would search diligently to find just the right fabric to make new seat covers for the chairs when needed. I have managed to hold on to one of the chairs to this date.

If we had used the front room for the sick room, the sleeping arrangements would not have been so messed up for everybody.

Sometimes I would have to go across the street and sleep with neighbor children, three of us in a bed. Usually it was on weekends when Ma's siblings from North Carolina would come to visit.

My sister was not yet three years old when all of this took place. She and Pa developed a close relationship. He would take her out for walks. We had a dog named Poochie. Poochie followed them everywhere they went. Whenever you saw Poochie you knew one of them was nearby. Pa also nicknamed my sister. He called her by the name of "Sugerbuger." That name stuck with her for as long as anyone was alive who remembered Pa and spent time with them. Folk also talked about her blue eyes. She and my brother both have blue eyes. My eyes are green and did not draw attention.

Pa had a radio that he had moved over to Ma's sick room. It was a floor console model and stood about three plus feet high and was about thirty inches wide. He would sit in there and listen to news and play music. When no one else was in the room I would go in to sit with Ma. I would play with the radio, trying the different stations. One day something big happened to me. I heard Elvis Pressley for the first time and I was a lifetime fan after that. I had to keep quiet about it because church folk were disgusted with the hip movements. I did not let anyone know that I listened to the radio whenever I could get time alone in the sick room. I did not let my parents know why, but I did manage to go to a neighbor's house when Elvis appeared on the Ed Sullivan show.

Ma had a condition back then that was called dropsy. Today we know that condition to be congestive heart failure. There was a Dr. Turner in Greenwood who would come out to the village and check on Ma ever so often. He would bring special medications with him. And he would also get my mother to fix foods for Ma that were salt free. That was about all that was done for the condition back then. Ma's legs continued to get larger from the fluid backup and her breathing became more labored. When Ma's sisters and brother would come in from the mountains to visit, they would frequently bring crops and foods that they had back in the mountains to help with our family meals during the week.

My mother labored intensely to fix all the right foods as the doctor would tell her to do. She was careful to make dishes as salt free as possible. On one of the visits from the mountain siblings, Aunt Monte took my mother aside and told her not to work so hard with all of those salt free dishes because Ma did not have much time left to live and let's feed her the foods she liked most. After that point, my mother started fixing regular food again and Ma ate what we ate. Often that would be fatback, gravy biscuits, grits, and when we could afford it we had bacon. As time moved on, Ma ate less and less. In her final days, she ate nothing at all.

Sometimes Dad's sister, Aunt Ruth would come over and stay at the house to help. My cousin Lonnie would come with her. Lonnie was a very sensitive child and was easily frightened. My Mom enjoyed pulling pranks on him and frightening him to tears. One evening, after dark, Mom went outside and got a ladder up to the window and started making ghostly noises and Lonnie went into near convulsions. Mom thought it was funny and I did not know what to think. Lonnie was disturbed about that for years.

In Ma's later days, various family members would come in and sit up with Ma in the sick room. I was spending more and more time across the street sleeping with my friends. One Sunday, when I came home from church my Mom met me at the door and sent me across the street to sit on our neighbor's porch. The mother of my friends came out and sat on the front porch with me. She told me that Ma had passed away. We sat there and talked, until finally a big black car came to my house across the street and Ma's body was taken out of our house.

Much commotion started taking place at my house with many people coming and going. There was a constant stream of folk bringing food. Family members started piling in. There was much crying. Everybody had an opinion about what was to be done about the funeral. Then the discussion started about what we would wear to the funeral. My Dad and Pa got some control over the discussions. The next day, they went into town to the funeral home and made all of the arrangements. When that was over, some orderliness prevailed in the house.

On the second day after Ma died, my mother loaded me in the car and we drove into town. She carried me into a dress shop and bought me a new dress to wear to the funeral. I had never owned a dress quite like this one, a store-bought dress. The design was far different from the home-made clothes we wore. Most of all, it was unusual that Mom went into the store with me.

My mother had been the primary person taking care of Ma during her illness in our home. After Ma passed away, my mother was pushed to the background and had little input into what would be done. Shortly after we got home from town with my new dress, the living room furniture had to be completely rearranged. I did not understand why but soon after the rearrangement of the furniture, the hearse arrived at our house with a coffin containing Ma's body. The undertakers came in and took over the arrangement of the room. There was a stand with a sign-in book placed on the porch at the front door along with a white wreath. On the far end of the living room was the casket with flowers on each side.

A silence came over the house and everybody in the house came to the front room and looked down toward the coffin. The undertakers, in very slow motion, raised the lid on the coffin. Everybody in the room was given the opportunity to come to the coffin and look at Ma. I remember going up to the coffin and peeking in and quickly returning to the other side of the room. Some of the folk that looked inside of the coffin cried and wailed. My mother took a position sort of out of the way of everybody and I do not recall her going to the coffin and looking in.

As it started getting dark that night, discussions were constant about who was going to sit up with Ma in the living room. During all of this, many of our church friends were coming and going with gracious food. I went across the street and stayed with my friends again that night. The next day was the funeral. There was much hullabaloo about the meal that would be there in the house before and after the funeral. I got dressed, and waited and waited before we left for the church. It seems there was much food coming in, many folk eating, and few to help with the clean-up. The clean-up always fell on my mother.

Before we went to the church, the funeral home folk came and closed the coffin and carried it to the church which was about two blocks away. The family all traveled by car over to the church. The undertaker lined us up outside and we marched in to reserved seats. Ma's coffin was down front and open. There was music, solo singing, and the preacher preached. There was much weeping and wailing. When the preacher was finished, the funeral director asked the family to stand and he directed us to the front to view Ma's body.

Ma's sister, Aunt Jessie, reached into the casket and pulled Ma up and hugged her and cried out loud. Everybody went down front to view Ma one last time.

When it was over, the funeral director and some men closed the coffin and carried it to the hearse. We all loaded in cars and followed over to Hillcrest Cemetery. All of the cars in the opposite lane from us would stop while the procession went by. Hillcrest Cemetery was over at the Greenwood Mill Village near Lowell Street and Mathis Avenue. Hillcrest Cemetery was a cemetery where persons and families who had worked at Greenwood Mill could be buried for free. It was in the middle of pasture land. At the graveside, the preacher started preaching again and I just watched the cows move around and moo.

When we got back to the house, there was another round of funeral food. The folk from out of town were getting things together and packing up. When they all left, my Dad and Pa started the first of many lengthy conversations about "what next?" My mother was glad when all of the company was gone.

My mother seemed to get tense and hyper at times about all that had taken place. Not only had she been the caregiver for a dying person, but she also had to host all of the company that came and went during the season of dying. Mom had a very traumatic childhood filled with much loss. She had never reconciled her own losses, and now with so much grief all around her, the survivor in her took two paths. One was the sweet loving person in public. Everyone in the church loved the kind gentle ways they observed. The other path was a raging inferno that only a few came to know.

Mom did not like living in the house where Ma had died. Relocation was the next thing on her agenda.

CHAPTER SIX

BEACON STREET

AFTER MA DIED, MY MOTHER insisted on moving about two blocks from where we lived. A village house had become available that was just like the one we had been living in on Lanett Street. The house was across the street from one of the side entrance walkways to the mill. We moved up there before I entered the seventh grade. The 107 Beacon Street house had central heat also. I do not think I realized what a blessing it was to have good heat even when I heard others complain about being cold. By this time, Pa was living with us. The property on Laurel Road had been sold.

In the summer, it was very hot and we continued to have no air-conditioning, but finally got a window fan. It did not make much difference. Supposedly it was to work by turning the fan on exhaust and slightly raise the windows so that a draft would be created through the house. Some nights the heat was unbearable inside the house. We kids would take a quilt out into the yard and lay it on the grass, and sleep out there all night. One thing the village houses had was a screened-in back porch. We would move our kitchen table out to the screened porch in the summer and eat our meals out there. The church did not have air conditioning either, but the funeral homes would give hand held cardboard fans to the churches. I would sometimes bring a fan home from church and sit on the porch and fan myself.

Mom still maintained a formal dining room. It became what I called the nose punishment room. Sometimes we would be punished for our misbehavior by having to stand so many minutes in the corner with our nose facing into the corner. Occasionally my brother and I both would be in a corner at the same time. The dining room still could have been better used as an additional bedroom.

The Beacon Street house was on a lot that sloped downward from front to back, with only two steps onto the porch in the front. What we called the back porch off the kitchen was actually on the side of the house. The kitchen door was about half way down the length of the house. There were five steps down to get out the back door. If you left the back-door steps and walked to the back corner, you continued to go down slope. On the back side of the house was the opening to the underpin or crawl space. The wooden door that opened into the crawl space was four plus feet high and you could walk in on ground level and stand up.

On Lanett Street, there had been five steps onto the front porch with three steps out the back door onto a level lot. The door to the underpin was in the same place but it was about two feet tall at best. You had to bend over to gain entrance and at the same time placing one foot a few inches below the door opening onto the dirt and then bring in the other foot. It was easier to move around under the Lanett house the further you trekked to the space under the front porch. The crawl space under the front of the house did not require so much bending over. Because of the difficulty of access very little could be stored under the Lanett Street house. An adult would have to crawl on their knees to get around. However, it was a good hiding place for a short person.

Due to the ease of access to the space under the Beacon Street house, Pa stored some of his keepsakes from Laurel Road, after it was sold, in the underpin. I was always fascinated with his camel-back or curved dome-lid steamer trunk. Many times, I found the door to the crawl space open and Pa would be sitting at his trunk with the lid open. Sometimes he would be going through things in the upper tray. Other times the tray would be sitting on the side and he would be going through belongings in the bottom. I was allowed to sit, watch, and talk to him while he worked his trunk, but somehow, I knew not to look inside. It did hold a long tress of hair that I would see him hold up sometimes.

The crawl space at Beacon Street was not a special play space for me as the Lanett Street crawl space had been. By the time we got to Beacon Street, I no longer needed a safe place like I had at Lanett Street.

Most of the kids in church who were the ages of my brother and I were taking piano lessons. One girl got so good she even played at church sometimes. We did not have a piano but with my delivering papers I thought I could make enough money to pay for piano lessons. Somehow a piano appeared in our living room. There was a story about it being a hand me down from somebody. I always wondered if Pa had gotten it for us. His mantel clock was placed on top of the piano.

My brother and I did start piano lessons. My sister was only five years old, not in school, and she did not take lessons. By the end of the school year, I was beginning to play chords with my left hand. My brother was still playing with just his right hand. At the Spring recital, I played a piece that was about thirty bars long. A six-bar piece repeating the same three notes was played by my brother. It was called 'Blackie and Whittie' alternating the striking of the white keys and the black keys. He was laughed at and humiliated. He never touched the piano again.

After Pa moved in with us, Ruby was divorced again. She would come over and always tried to get money from Pa. Sometimes she would have a new boyfriend with her and this would make my mother very angry, as well as Pa. Pa knew how to deal with his frustrations but my Mom was always left loaded and ready to lash out. Pa frequently took long walks and that is how he seemed to quiet his anxiety.

Pa was also trying to help out my Mom with the grocery cost. I do not know where he got his money but he frequently bought bacon and ham for us. The bacon was very special and it was essentially rationed out. When available we could have one piece each at a meal. We begged for more but never got it. The extra pieces were held back with several biscuits for Pa to have during the day. I used to break my piece of bacon into several pieces and show my brother that I had more than one piece on my plate. He would get upset and the family got upset with me for tricking him. It took him a while to figure out how I got more pieces.

This was the year we got a modern looking, up-to-date car. The pharmacist who ran the grocery-drug store in the Village Shopping Center put his green and white Chevrolet station wagon up for sale. My Dad worked out a deal, and it was exciting to ride around in such a good-looking car. It was the vehicle in which I would learn to drive.

Back then, in the state of South Carolina, a person could get a learner's permit to drive, sixty days before the fourteenth birthday. A licensed adult had to be in the car with you at all times when using your learner's permit. Mine was obtained right on that sixtieth day. Before I got my learner's permit, I had observed all of the coordination it took to change gears and use the clutch. I wondered if I could ever do all of that in sync. I learned to drive very quickly since our new car was automatic. I drove only on the village with one of my parents.

Then the day came when my Mom wanted something from Langley's grocery store—now three blocks away since we moved to Beacon Street. Mom told me to just take the car and go to the store. She said I would be okay. As I was leaving the village street to cross the railroad track to go to Langley's, a policeman pulled me over. He said I ran a stop sign when I came off the village street over to the railroad track.

I did have my permit with me and it was obvious no one was in the car with me. I did not argue. I was terrified and unnerved because people were watching. I do not recall anything about the conversation with the officer. But I do remember driving back home with a ticket and telling my Mom. The ticket was actually made out to her for "allowing a minor to operate a vehicle." She and my Dad took care of that and there was no more driving alone. We were living in Anderson when I obtained my full driver's license.

By the time we were living on Beacon Street, my brother and I were considered of sufficient age that we could go out unaccompanied on Halloween. In earlier years, all we could do was go with a parent to the carnival held at the school. On the mornings after Halloween, you could see all of the deeds of the mischief-makers from the night before. Cars would be marked all over with soap. The windows at the shopping center had writings all over them. Trash cans would be turned over. On our first night out on the streets, we did not tarry long. Some of the more experienced tricksters tried to spook us and we had already promised Dad we would not do bad things.

Back then, there were no preventive vaccines for measles, mumps, and chickenpox. There were two kinds of measles. My brother and I had all of these as they moved through the village. My brother had a longer time than usual with a high fever when he had measles. He also developed a throat coated in white. The doctor came to the house to check on him. He got okay but later in high school, it was discovered he had a heart valve defect. I did wonder about this as I went on to nursing school in my twenties. I had a long bout with mumps that I remember was painful. Chickenpox left us all with scars where we scratched the itching places. I do not recall my sister having these sicknesses at Harris. She did not catch them from being in the house with us.

We were a little closer to the church when we lived on Beacon Street. We all went to church as usual on Sunday mornings. Pa did not like Sunday School. However, he would come to preaching every Sunday. When my brother and I would get out of Sunday School we would hurry to the auditorium and sit with Pa. He had a regular seat closer to the back. Mom and Dad always sat closer to the front.

Pa shared a bedroom with my brother. One Saturday night, Pa wanted to show me something in his closet. He opened the closet door and pulled his gray coat off of the nail on which it hung. It was a gray hobo style blazer and he wore it every day, summer or winter. He opened up the inside of the jacket and pulled out some folded papers that were in the right inside breast pocket. He told me these were his important papers and if anything happened to him, I was to let my Dad know where these papers were. I assured him I would do just that, even though the conversation made me ill at ease.

The next morning at church, my brother and I waited for Pa to arrive for preaching. He never showed up. After church, my sister and brother were ahead of me running up the sidewalk to get home to see where Pa was and why he did not come to church. By the time I got in the back door, they were already running down the hallway calling "Pa, Pa." I was about ten feet behind them. I could see his feet on the corner of the bed as I got closer to the door. His feet were not moving. By the time I got fully in the doorway, I could see he was dead. My brother and sister ran out the back door calling for Mom and Dad who were coming up the sidewalk. I just stood frozen in the hall. Dad rushed in and went back there, looked and told me to run and get Mr. Styron.

My mind was rushed with the immediate events, and bombarded by what Pa had told me the night before. I tried to tell my Dad what Pa had said but he rushed me out the door to get Mr. Styron. Mr. Styron was Dad's spiritual mentor.

I ran through the alleyway to Mr. Styron's house. I beat on the back door and told him what had happened. Mr. Styron told me to get in his car and we would drive to Beacon Street. When we arrived, Dad was calling the doctor. Dr. Turner said he was coming to the house. Finally, I got my Dad to listen to me about what Pa had said the night before. Dad did go to the closet and found the papers in Pa's gray coat pocket. Then Mom called our neighbors from Lanett Street, the Thomas family. My brother, sister, and I were sent to their house.

The Thomas house had a swing on the front porch and we played in the swing and around the porch most of the afternoon. My sister went across the street and played with the Thomas's granddaughter who was her same age. It seemed like we played there for hours. I made everybody uncomfortable when another neighbor came over and I informed them that Pa had died. I left them speechless when I brought it up. Finally, Mr. Bud noticed the hearse was leaving the village. Then, we were allowed to go home. We got my five-year-old sister from across the street and the three of us walked back up to Beacon Street.

Pa had died on a Sunday just as Ma had died on a Sunday, one year, one month, and ten days earlier. My father was thirty-three years old when he buried his mother, and now was thirty-four years old and burying his father. The deep-rooted seeds of steadiness planted in my Dad by his Dad were now called to bear.

The weight of managing a heavy flow of people in and out for the next week fell on my Mom once again. Her main desire was for the casket not to be brought to the home this time. She was obliged and the casket was placed in the front of the church before the funeral and closed before the funeral started. Pa did have some out of town family to attend the funeral, and some of Ma's family came also. Many friends from Greenwood Mill and friends from our church were in and out. There was no big fuss this time about what we would wear to the funeral. The funeral food brigade was in full force once again. We did manage to have a few meals in that formal dining room.

My brother had shared the bedroom with Pa but he did not start back sleeping in there again until after the funeral. My mother felt this was not a good thing. Once again, she activated her campaign about our needing to move to another place. She just did not want us to live in a house where someone had died.

Soon after the funeral was over, questions were raised about the people that showed up and did not sit with the family, but told some they were kin to Pa. No one knew who they were. They did not tarry long after the funeral. However, the discussions went on for months. Many of the discussions went on at our kitchen table, after my bedtime, when they thought I was asleep. I could hear Uncle Fred, Lindsey, and Aunt Ruth discussing something serious with Mom and Dad about that woman. She was seen parked in a car in front of our house for a few hours one night.

At some point, Dad and I went under the house and went through Pa's trunk. Some papers were of interest to my Dad. The only thing that caught my attention was the long tress of dark brown hair. The piece of hair and a few other items in the trunk raised Uncle Fred's curiosity. He went up to Big Creek community in Fannin County, Georgia, and felt he confirmed that Pa had another relationship before meeting Ma. There was speculation that the person who had been seen in front of our house was the child of Pa, left behind when he departed Fannin County. Pa had left Big Creek Church Community when he found his then wife in bed with his best friend. I will always wonder if Ma ever knew about that history. I heard the story many years later from one of Pa's cousins who still lived on the Tipton property. The fifty years later version was drama filled.

When it looked like we were not going to get another house on the Harris Mill village, Mom started talking about Dad finding another job. In the Fall after Pa died, I entered the eighth grade at the junior high school. My brother was in the sixth grade at Harris elementary and our sister, Ann, entered the first grade. This was the beginning of a sad story for my baby sister. She began a journey of being in a different school or house almost every year of her school days. The distresses attached to so much moving around were never addressed since the motto of our Mom was "forget the past, you never have to think about it."

One of my Dad's high school and textile league baseball buddies, Pratt, worked in the shipping department of the Greenwood Mill. He was in and out of our place once or twice a month. Dad was his equivalent at Harris Mill. Pratt had become restless in Greenwood and sought similar work from another textile firm in Anderson, South Carolina. Pratt was at our home one weekend and revealed his relocation plans. My Mom jumped on that.

Mom started up with Dad about seeing if Pratt could get him a job in Anderson. Anytime Mom heard that Pratt was going to be back in town for a weekend, he always got an invitation for a meal. Even though we did not have much money for food, my Mom was well known for her biscuits and gravy. Mom started making hints to Pratt about our needing to move and get away from Greenwood. I guess it was inevitable that by the close of my eighth-grade Pratt had found a job for my Dad in Anderson with the M. Lowenstein Company that had bought out the Orr Cotton Mill along with the Lyons Synthetic Division in Anderson. The job was in the payroll department of the corporate office in Anderson.

CHAPTER SEVEN

DAD THINGS

MY DAD WAS A FUN-LOVING person and wanted my brother and I to have fun also. He taught us how to preserve the chalk, draw and play hopscotch on the sidewalk. We both got bicycles at appropriate times around first grade and third grade. My brother's bike had training wheels. We always had roller skates that had a key to keep them tightened around the toe of our shoes. While many of the kids were getting go-carts of sorts, we could not afford one. Dad took some scrap wood he got from the mill and built a large box and took apart our skates and nailed them down to the bottom of the box and we could roll down the hill in our "roller box." And, we did get new skates.

Playing marbles was a favorite back then. My brother was more interested in playing marbles than I was. It must have been a guy thing. There were special types of marbles to obtain and a special cloth sack to carry them in. The game carried emotion with it because you either won or lost your marbles.

We lived in a house with a large yard beside us which we kept cut, on the corner of Lanett and Hutson Streets. Kids would gather on the lot to play backer sac. Backer sac was played like baseball but with a ball made from a stuffed tobacco sack. The bat was a cut limb from a tree about the size of a walking cane. When tobacco sacks were hard to come by, we would take a sock and stuff it part way with a rag or old socks, tie a knot into it and pull the excess ribbing of the sock across the knot. Because the ball was soft, it was thrown at and had to strike the runner for an out. Dad never played backer sac but he sure did enjoy advising the game.

In the Spring of each year, we would make our own kites. Some of the kids got a store-bought kite but Dad taught us how to make ours. We would first make glue from a paste of flour and water and let it set up while we got everything else together. We would cut some sticks from the woods and get them tied into position where they crossed over. On the end of each stick, we would cut out a wedge. We had carefully cut sheets of newspaper. After running string around the edges of the sticks and embedding it into the wedged-out places, we pulled tightly getting one side to bow out. Then we would tie it off. Next, we tied a string from one side to the other side of the short stick. We would then lay the bowed-out side down on top of the newspaper sheets and cut paper about two inches out from the string all way around. Then we would fold newspaper over the string, and with our paste we would glue the edge down across the string.

After letting the kite dry out for a day, we tied a narrow strip of cloth from the bottom for a tail. From the crossing of the two sticks which were about three quarters of the way up from the tail, we attached a ball of string which we had rolled onto a spool. Thus, we had a kite. During the last Spring my Dad was alive, our son came up to visit, carried Dad outside in his wheelchair and together they flew a kite.

Occasionally Dad would take us to a drive-in-movie theater in the evening to watch a cowboy movie or comedy. There was a playground area in front of where the cars parked and we would play before the movie started. We would bring our own food because the price at the drive-in-movie food bar was too high. Previews would start and we would run to the car and place the speaker on the inside of a window and watch the movie. On one trip to the drive-in, a car hit us from behind as we were waiting to make the left turn off Highway 25. Dad's knee hit the gear shift and it bothered him for a few weeks. No one else in the car was injured. Mom was always afraid to make left turns after the incident. Cars did not have signal lights for turning back then. Turn signals were given by the driver holding their arm out the window.

Along with my Mom developing a fear of left turns, I developed a fear of going across a wooden bridge. It is a wonder Dad took us anywhere. To get to my Aunt Ruth's house, we had to cross over a rickety wooden bridge. Before getting there, my Mom always started talking about whether it would still be standing. If it was standing, she worried if it would hold us. Then there was the story from my Uncle Jack that the bridge had been down for a few days, and he needed to get across. He put boards across it for each tire to ride on and did get across. I always wondered how he kept the tires aligned on the boards. Somehow, I outgrew my fear of wooden bridges, even though there were many wooden bridges in those days.

Horses continually got my Dad's attention. I always wonder if it was from watching all of the cowboy movies when he worked in the theater. Dad met a man that worked in the Harris Mill who lived out in the country. His family had several horses and boarded a few for others. There was a fenced in track for the horses. Frequently we would visit the track and watch the horses. Dad would describe the different types of walks and gaits the horses would get into. He seemed pleased when I finally became able to identify the gaits. Occasionally he would mention how he would like to get us a horse and we could board it with his friend.

Every year when the county fair opened, we always went and Dad spent much time with us explaining all of the livestock. At school, we were given free tickets to get into the fair but there was not much money to do the rides. Perhaps that is why we spent so much time looking at the livestock and the various contest winners for cooking, sewing, canning and various crafts.

My father must have soaked up every word he was taught in school. He had so much knowledge about so many things. When walking anywhere, he could make a major life lesson out of almost everything he would see on the way. He knew much about trees, shrubs, and creatures. I learned all of the preferences for various shrubs and flowers to have a beautiful yard.

Dad also learned Pig Latin along the way and taught it to all of us. According to the dictionary, Pig Latin is a made-up language formed from English by transferring the initial consonant or consonant cluster of each word to the end of the word and adding a vocalic syllable (usually 'pig ˌlatn: so *chicken soup* would be translated to *ickenchay oupsay*). Pig Latin is typically spoken playfully, as if to convey secrecy. Even into Dad's sixties and seventies, some of our family gatherings would go into Pig Latin just to see who could still remember how.

On one occasion, we noticed a few beautiful yellow monarch butterflies. When we got home, Dad got a fruit jar and lid and we hung out in the yard until we saw one in our shrubbery. He captured the butterfly. Then he gave me a small piece of cloth with some alcohol on it. In a very slow motion, he opened the jar and took hold of the butterfly with both wings between his thumb and index finger. Then I was instructed to place the tip of the cloth on the nose of the butterfly. The butterfly died very quickly. We spread the butterfly out on a piece of paper. The next day we went into town and bought a special type of glue and a small frame where the glass beveled out. We mounted and framed the butterfly. I had a science project that lasted for years. Catching the butterfly in the jar was the same technique he taught us for catching bumble bees.

I also learned about June bugs from him. If you ever saw one on its back, it could not turn itself over and fly away. Occasionally there would be one on our front porch. When on its back, the June bug would kick its legs up in the air. Dad taught me how to make a lasso loop from a piece of thread. I could lasso one leg and turn the bug over and it would try to fly away. For a few minutes, you would have a flying toy on the string. However, you always ended up losing the grip on your string and the bug toy got away.

Comic books were a big thing back then. My Dad would find a way to buy one every now and then. He enjoyed reading them to us. We always had a few on hand but never the stacks of comic books like some of our friends had. Keeping up with baseball and boxing was also a favorite pastime.

Many of our walks on the village involved going to visit the sick and shut-ins. Often one of our neighbors would also accompany the visitation. Dad was sensitive to the sick folk. One Saturday, my brother and I went with him to the Shriners Hospital in Greenville to visit the daughter of one of our church members. She had a deformity that was corrected with several surgeries. I had never been in a building with a round room. Her bed was one of many in the round room which also had many windows.

Dad enjoyed his work at the mill. However, living at the "Harris Mill" was constantly being corrected to "Harris Plant." Since the manufacturing facility named, Harris, did not run cotton, some thought it was a step up from the cotton mills. Manufacturing of nylon fabric carried more clout for some. The job expectations were clear for each day. Dad enjoyed delivering on all of the daily expectations. The last part of his daily job was taking the outgoing mail from the plant down to the village post office every afternoon. The post office was operated by Frances Gunnels who was like a grandmother to every child on the village. We would all stop in and tell her hello several times a week. In the summer months, the plant had softball teams and Dad enjoyed playing softball with his work buddies.

My Dad was a very steady and stable person as his father had been. He could be counted on to do what he said he would do. Even when other family members made bad decisions and had to live out the consequences, they were still his family. He stopped short of enabling his brother and sisters but never closed the door to listening to issues. My mother felt put upon by them and never wanted anything to do with them unless they lived by her standards.

Dad often told the story about Ma and Pa making the decision to take Fred from Greenwood back to the mountains because Fred had become so active with the unions who were trying to organize the mills in the early 1930s. Ma had feared for Fred's life and wanted to protect him from himself. Dad seemed to think that rescue was needed because of the level of violence at the mills. Fred was also known for his boxing talent. Boxing matches were set up after each of the textile baseball games at the Greenwood Mills ball park.

Dad was the only one of the siblings to complete high school. He did graduate from Greenwood High School, which was eleven years back then for completion. Often schools would be closed in October for a few weeks when the farmers needed help with picking the cotton.

Much discipline was exercised by Dad in early years as evidenced by his success in playing high school football and textile league baseball. Not only did the Cincinnati Reds talk with him before he was drafted in World War II, they also approached him when he returned from the Army. He served as a paratrooper in Special Operations behind the lines in France and Germany and is listed in the Roll Call of the Airborne and Special Operations Museum located at Ft. Bragg, North Carolina.[3]

One could say that whether Dad's personality was inherited or acquired is irrelevant because it got the job of life and living done very well. My take is that his strength was delivered to him daily by the goodness of God that flowed through the servants of God that came across his path each day. Dad's part was opening himself up for God's goodness to flow. Dad knew he was dependent on God. He made himself an open vessel to receive God's goodness and to pass it along as it had been given to him.

Cotton was a big crop in my younger days. Whenever we drove by a cotton field near picking time, it looked like a sea of white. Dad

3   https://www.asomf.org/rollcall_registrants/tipton-edward/?_sfm_rc_last_name=Tipton.

always reminded us of how the cotton gave jobs to so many folk, and the cotton had built the industry that even now employed him and gave us a house in which to live. Several weeks later we would see folk in the fields picking the cotton. He and Mom were grateful they no longer had to pick cotton.

CHAPTER EIGHT

MY MOTHER IN GREENWOOD

MY MOTHER, MATTIE LOU MARETT Tipton, was born in Fair Play, South Carolina, in 1925. Her parents were Evangeline Stamps Marett (1899-1966) and Talmadge D. Marett (1894-1930). Her father was a veteran of World War I and he was exposed to mustard gas. He was on the western front when German soldiers first fired the lethal gas in 1917. Talmadge returned to Fair Play with respiratory problems.

The Marett family was a large farm family in the Fair Play community. The farm provided Talmadge work as he was able. The Stamps family was from the Anderson, South Carolina, area. My mother was one of four siblings, all girls, born within a six-year time frame after her Dad came home from the war.

As the story was told, my Mom was four when her father was found dead in the corn field in the heat of the day. Her Mom could not cope with the loss and the family dynamics. She abandoned her children and went to Newnan, Georgia. The siblings of her father swapped the children around and a decision was made. The four girls were loaded up and taken to the Connie Maxwell Baptist Orphanage in Greenwood, South Carolina. Later, the word Orphanage was changed to Children's Home. My Mom was next to the youngest. She and her baby sister stayed there until completion of high school.

After several years, when Evangeline, my grandmother, had a stable job in a cotton mill in Newnan, she came to the orphanage and got the two older sisters and carried them back to Georgia to live with her. They stayed with her and worked until they became of age to join the Women's Army Corps (WAC) during World War II. They went into the WAC around the same time that their mother, Evangeline, was admitted to the Milledgeville State Hospital in Milledgeville, Georgia, for long term treatment of mental illness. The older sisters would occasionally visit the younger sisters at the orphanage, bring them clothes and candy, and keep them updated about their mother. The abandonment issues followed the four siblings for the rest of their lives.

The orphanage knew how to keep everybody task oriented, and busy with the demands of cooking and sewing for their residential cottage. The girls also had to take turns doing the sewing for the boys' cottages as the boys took turns stoking the furnaces for the girls' cottages. From my mother's stories, there must have been rules for everything.

The anchor and solace for orphanage life was the Baptist church. The Baptist pastor for the orphanage church set the tone. He knew how to solicit support from other churches in the community and was able to acquire government rationed foods for the children. Some of the life lessons taught by the pastor were recorded in a book entitled, "Consider the Parasite" by A.T. Jamison in 1934. Near the closing of her life my Mom gave me her copy of Dr. Jamison's book.

Connie Maxwell had its own elementary school. The high school grades were completed at Greenwood High School, and that's where my Mom and Dad met. When the orphans completed high school, they could no longer live at the orphanage. They had to find jobs and a place to live. Many went into military service. My Mom's younger sister passed the test to get into the Navy and the Navy nurses training. My Mom could not pass the math part of the testing for admission. She was a year behind my Dad in high school, and he had already been drafted into the Army when she got out of high school.

A social worker at the orphanage named Sybil Foster helped my Mom find a job working in the dining room at High Hampton Inn in Cashiers, North Carolina. Housing was provided for the workers. When my Dad completed his paratrooper training at Ft. Benning, Georgia, he went to High Hampton Inn to find my Mom and to get married. They resided near Ft. Bragg, North Carolina, until my Dad shipped out to the European theater. When Dad left to go overseas, he made arrangements for my Mom to live with his parents at Greenwood Mill. When he shipped out, my Mom was pregnant with me.

The Connie Maxwell Orphanage bordered the back side of Greenwood Mill Village so it was not a strange place for my Mom. Mom had to learn to live within a family unit for the first time. Life was not orderly and structured for her like at the orphanage. Life was not a matter of complying with the rules and routines set by others. Years later she did express her struggle trying to exist in the same house with so many dynamics out of her control. When Dad returned from Europe, he got a job and they moved into an apartment. Mom did learn what it took to please people and how to say the right things when in public. Often, she told the story about trying to run away from the orphanage.

One time, as she was walking the train tracks heading out of Greenwood, there was a big, serious moment of shock. Many times, Mom told the story about how she came to realize she had nowhere to go and no one wanted her. She was filled with sudden warmth, realizing she had a Heavenly Father. Her Heavenly Father did want her, and her Heavenly Father had provided His servants to care for her at the orphanage. She returned to the orphanage. The teachings of the church pastor, Dr. Jamison, began to guide her life. She accepted Christ as her Savior and was baptized at the Connie Maxwell Baptist Church.

When telling this story about deciding not to run away from the orphanage, Mom always drew much sympathy. She knew how to maximize sympathy from anyone willing to listen. At the Harris Baptist Church, she worked with a girls group older than me. She always had them feeling sorry for orphans. On the positive side, she could woo others to an awareness of the less fortunate and support for the underdog.

My Mom also developed a fan club for her cooking. Cooking and sewing were major skills she brought with her from the orphanage. Eating her biscuits and gravy could make folk feel like they had enjoyed a full meal. The aroma of the fresh baked biscuits lingered for hours. She was just as talented with any other groceries that came our way. In summertime, she often sent me to a friend's house that was about a half mile from the mill village. I always thought it was for fun and play. However, these folk always planted a large garden. Without my knowledge, I was being volunteered to come help them pick the garden, and in turn would be able to bring home a big basket of free vegetables. It seemed like hard work back then but was major education for me. I learned about gardening and how to preserve vegetables for the winter months with the canning process. It had a big payoff for me in later years, being able to grow foods and preserve them for the winter.

There was also a lady, Azalee Harmon, in the church that lived off the village. Azalee had a beauty shop in her house. My Mom offered me to her as a cleaning person to keep her yard swept and the kitchen clean. Because I did that work we got free haircuts from her. Mrs. Harmon also taught me how to ring a chicken's neck. She finished up early in the shop one day and came out to the yard where we caught a chicken. She showed me how to ring the neck, dip the dead chicken into boiling water, pluck the feathers, clean the bird, and end up with fried chicken on the table for supper. I never did that again.

One of my Mom's favorite foods was pineapple sandwiches. During the war, cans of pineapple were rationed. Anytime she had the money, she would buy a can of pineapple and we would have pineapple sandwiches with lots of mayonnaise and listen to the memory of the rationing of pineapple. Sometimes if we had no pineapple we would make mayonnaise sandwiches with lots of mayo and nothing else. Personally, my Dad and I preferred tomato sandwiches.

We also did a lot of scavenging for fabric to make our clothes. Many times, folk that had animals would buy feed in sacks that were made of fabric. We were always on the lookout for folk who may be discarding the feed sacks. We would wash the fabric sacks and make them into a skirt. When we had money, we would buy finished cloth in town. I do not recall how my brother got his clothes.

The way of the orphanage was deeply seated in my Mom's thinking. She was preoccupied when we lived on Lanett Street that my brother and I had to have a play table like they had at the orphanage. At the orphanage, six to eight children would sit around a play table and do homework or color. There was no let up until my Dad got a four by eight-foot sheet of plywood and built us such a table. She painted it blue and it was placed in the corner of a bedroom and took up the major space of the room. It was rarely used but Mom showed it off, and bragged to all who visited that her children had a play table. However, the play table did not make it to Beacon Street. As we got older, she had the same obsession that we needed a four-foot wide desk each. She asked a man in the church to build the desks for us. Unlike the play table, the desks went with us through high school.

Sometimes my Mom would take me out to the orphanage and leave me for a weekend. I never did understand this. It was awkward for me. She said I needed to know what it was like. My brother never had to go. I would stay in the cottage where my Mom was raised, and with one of the house parents that knew my Mom. It did expose me to her heritage. Sometimes we would pick up one of the orphans and keep them in our house for a weekend.

For the most part, Mom was able to manage her life on the village and in the church. Doing things in town were difficult for her. She would drive us into town but she never got out. My brother or I were sent in to pick up the items she wanted. She did not interface with store clerks. Sometimes we would go in and pay one dollar on an account she had. When needing items at the A & P Grocery Store, we were sent in to do the shopping, and had to come out and wait on her to come pick us up. The waits did get long at times.

My mother's sweet and kind ways could easily turn into rage. Only a few people knew about her anger. She would beat me at times and it took me a few years to learn how to protect myself. I think at first other people noticed the bruises and marks on my body before I realized their presence. I became fixated on avoiding her when she was upset. I found a place of escape in the underpin or crawl space of our house. I would crawl under there and stay for hours. I had an imaginary playhouse under there and could hide behind a brick pillar and she could not see me from the entrance. There was not enough headroom for her to come into the crawl space. Sometimes I would sob and sigh about what had happened. I just could not figure out why she did it. After all, she would tell me she loved me and that I was her favorite child. When my Dad would get home, he would come to the entrance and call for me to come out. I felt safe when he was home. We would go for a walk or I would accompany him on an errand.

My brother would get spankings but I only recall him being spanked with a switch from a spirea bush. A twenty to twenty-five-inch branch would be broken off and the foliage stripped off and then used. I was usually whipped with a leather belt. I was never around if my sister ever received a spanking.

When I was in the fifth grade, I had a moment of resolve about the whippings I received at the hands of my mother. They were becoming increasingly painful. She had started using the buckle end of the belt most of the time now. She would chase me all over the room when I tried to get away from her. If I ran to a corner, she would jump across the bed and start on me over in the corner. In my moment of resolve, I decided two things. First, I would never cry again as she whipped, and I would stand still.

My standing still and not crying enraged her more and she was physically moving all of her body, like convulsions, every time she slung the belt. I made a conscious decision to defend myself. While she was jumping up and down, I eased my foot over a few inches in a way that she would trip over it. It worked. She fell. She stopped. I had some control, and there were less beatings after that. When I did not cry, she was more out of control. I even told her I would never cry again when she whipped me. I do not know if she ever figured out why she started falling.

I did not figure it out until many years later that the markings on my body must have been why my Dad and I were always visiting my school teachers in their home. No one else on the village had to do that. I think my Dad tried to make up for my Mom's deeds. Sometimes he would go out of the way to buy me something special.

One Saturday, Dad carried me into town to the dime store. As we were walking around looking at things, I picked up a magazine about Elvis Pressley. He did not seem to mind me looking at it. Many of the church folk complained about Elvis and his hip gyrations. He did take the magazine away from me and gave it to the sales lady and paid thirty-five cents for the magazine about Elvis. He said it was mine. That excitement lingered for years. I had something nobody else had. Thirty-five cents was big money to me.

My Mom did take the responsibility of caring for Ma seriously, and she worked very hard at doing the cooking and extra laundry and cleaning chores. I think the work had its toll on her overall well-being. When my grandmother's relatives would come to visit, the extra load of the company stirred an agitation that was held in abeyance until they left. I stayed across the street with neighbors on the weekends during that time.

As the years moved on, my Mom made small circles of friends with those who always agreed with her. She stayed away from folk who did not agree with her. Being unable to handle any confrontation kept her circle of friends changing. When teaching Sunday School, she was offended if anyone asked questions. However, everywhere we lived she did seem to keep at least one friend for the duration.

CHAPTER NINE

FELTON BRIDGE ROAD

WHEN DAD ACCEPTED THE JOB in Anderson, he struggled to find an affordable rental property. Mill village houses were not provided to Lowenstein workers in Anderson. Lowenstein sold the mill houses after they bought the Orr-Lyons Mill several years earlier. Dad was working for the corporate offices of Lowenstein and they were adjacent to the Orr Mill on South Main Street, Anderson, South Carolina. After several weeks of exploring the area, Dad found a small brick rental house in a rural area. Back then it was called Felton Bridge Road. It is now known as Pearman Dairy Road. It was six miles one way to Dad's office. The closest grocery store was two and one-half miles from the house. The church we finally settled in was three miles from the house. We continued to live without air conditioning. While we were living there, the Hartwell Dam was being backed up and water eventually covered eighty-seven square miles with much of it coming near our place on Felton Bridge Road. Sometimes we would ride around and see if we could detect higher water levels in former fields and pastures.

Our move to Anderson was at my Mom's insistence to move out of the house where Pa had died. It was a move up in Dad's career and he did have the ability to adjust to changing relationships and circumstances. However, Mom lacked the skill to adjust to changing conditions and situations that she could not control. After living for eight years at Harris Mill Village where the church, the grocery store, and work were within walking distance, the cost of gasoline now became a weekly concern. With only one vehicle, every day had to be carefully planned. We did not have a washer which meant we had to plan for trips to a laundromat each week. Dad needed white dress shirts every day so planning for laundry trips was critical. Learning to starch and iron clothes was part of growing up for girls back then. Ironing dress shirts was not easy. Ironing cotton handkerchiefs was easy and I laugh today every time I think about the importance we placed on ironed handkerchiefs.

The move to Anderson took place the summer between my eighth and ninth grade. When I entered the ninth grade at McCants Junior High School, my brother entered the seventh grade. We were both in the same school. My sister entered the second grade at Centerville Elementary School. This was the beginning of my sister attending a new school almost every year of her school days and a different house every year.

Learning to get back and forth to school was a chore. It included walking a quarter mile to a school bus stop, changing buses at the nearby elementary school, and then getting delivered to the junior high school. The return home in the afternoon was equally as frustrating and it was all a hassle when the weather was bad.

I had the good fortune to meet someone in my class who went to the same church we started attending. She showed much kindness to this newcomer at church and at school. She, Doris, lived about two miles down the road on which my Dad drove home from work. Doris had a married sister who worked in downtown Anderson and lived across the road from Doris. Doris did not want to get home from school at the school bus delivery time because her Dad would make her work on their dairy farm. Doris worked out a plan to walk from the junior high school up to the library in downtown and do her homework before going home. Her sister would pick Doris up at the library when she got off work, and Doris would be too late getting home to have to do any farm chores. Doris talked me into joining her in her jaunts to the library.

When I went to the library in the afternoons with Doris, my Dad would pick me up at her house on his way home from work. By doing this, I avoided being home with my Mom who was so unpredictable. It gave me quality study time and access to much help from the librarians when I had questions. The librarians would also introduce me to additional content and showed me how to access even more materials. After I learned how to use the card catalogue and reference materials in the library, there was a subject I wanted to know more about, but I did not want anyone to know I was inquisitive.

I wanted to know more about human sexuality. Nothing was taught about it in school back then. The subject was taboo. My menses had commenced when I was in the sixth grade at Harris. My Mom was able to teach me how to maintain hygiene. We could not afford sanitary products but Mom showed me how they made their own products from rags when she lived in the orphanage. The pain was horrible and you always worried about having blood showing. When I could save up money, I would purchase sanitary pads.

At the library, I was able to find some materials on sexuality and how the sperm and the egg made a baby. What I did not understand was just how close you had to get to a guy to make a baby. I guess I never found a book about intercourse. It must have sent me into some sort of overload because I thought about it frequently. It caused me not to enjoy the spin the bottle game played at church socials. A guy would spin a bottle in the middle of a circle of girls and whichever girl it pointed to when the bottle stopped, had to go for a walk with the guy. Parents did fuss a lot about such a game being played at church parties for the young people.

Doris and I were in the youth choir at church and attended GAs. My brother and sister did okay in the new church participating in choir and Sunbeams and RAs. Dad enjoyed the men things at church; however, Mom had much difficulty adjusting to new groups from many backgrounds. Mom did try to work with one of the youth groups but became very dissatisfied and gave up the role. The first part of my Mom's life was regimented by the routines of Connie Maxwell Orphanage. After her marriage, life was regimented by mill village living, where everyone worked, shopped, and went to church at the same places. The new adjustments became a challenge for her.

A dear lady in the church, Mrs. Franklin, recognized my Mom's struggle and invested much time in helping my Mom engage a new way of thinking about life and living. She was indeed an authentic spiritual mentor for my Mom. She and Mom spent many hours in scripture study and prayer. Mrs. Franklin gave my Mom a small plastic replica of a loaf of bread which contained small cards with a Bible verse on them. We would all take out a card and read it every morning before breakfast. Mrs. Franklin made up for the deficit we were experiencing as a family unit when the church was no longer the way of life as it had been on the mill village. The rural church was very diverse with folk from all walks of life. Even though it was a good size church, there was not much unity in the community. Even after we moved from that church, Mrs. Franklin continued to mentor my Mom for as long as we were in Anderson. Again, the goodness of God was reaching me through His servant as she ministered to my Mom. Mrs. Franklin's son ended up becoming the president of one of the Baptist colleges in South Carolina.

A sad thing did happen to us while living on Felton Bridge Road. Not too long after we moved there, our dog, Poochie, was hit by a car. Dad carried Poochie to the vet and brought him back home with his broken leg bandaged. Dad was taught how to change the dressings. Poochie kept getting worse and one morning, there were worms in his wound so Dad carried him back to the vet and had him put to sleep. There was much angst about how we would pay the vet also. It was a very sad day. I stayed home while everybody else went to the vet with Poochie. I cried and cried on my bed with my head down in the pillow.

What I had forgotten about was that some of our friends from Greenwood were coming up that afternoon and bringing supper with them. While I was deep into my sobbing, I kept hearing knocks on the door and just was not going to get up from the bed. I could not quit crying and finally did go to the door crying full throttle. When they saw me, they all rushed to hug me and tried to find out what had happened. They were so very concerned about me and wanted to console me. The matron of the group had been my Sunday School teacher at Harris. She and her older daughter went to the kitchen to get the supper going and the dad and younger kids took me outside and we walked and talked about our new place. Finally, my family returned very saddened and seem relieved they did not have to go through the story again with our guests. Again, the goodness of God was present in my life that day in the midst of much sadness through the presence of His servants from Harris Baptist Church.

The big awkward dining room table we had at Harris did not make it to Anderson but those mahogany chairs did. They were placed throughout the house. Mom still wanted to keep a formal living room with no television. What should have been the third bedroom for my brother was made into a television room with him having a cot type of bed up against the wall where we sat to watch television in the day and served as his bed at night. Mom's sisters did visit occasionally and they got the beds and the kids got the floor.

I did not understand back then about grief responses. I guess I must have thought my Mom had the right idea after Ma passed away in 1957. We were not to cry or act like Ma's relatives from North Carolina had acted. It was to never be talked about. I am not sure if my deep reaction to Poochie having to be put to sleep, the intense crying and sobbing, had opened up unhealed wounds I was carrying about the loss of Ma and Pa. Ma had always been a kind, gentle, and loving person. Ma had a capacity for gentleness that my Mom knew nothing about. About a month after Poochie was gone, I started waking up during the night once or twice a month in a deep sob and heavy heartedness about Ma being gone. I would just lay very still in bed and try to figure out what was going on. Why was I crying and why did it hurt so bad? Morning would come and I would act like everything was okay.

I would ask to go back to Greenwood and visit with some of my friends at Harris. Mom would never go back to Harris, but occasionally Dad would take me to Harris when he went back to Greenwood to visit his siblings, Fred and Ruth. It was over fifty years later before I experienced that sense of unity in community like we had known at Harris.

I do not recall much about what was going on with my brother and sister while living on Felton Bridge Road. While there, my brother did complete his surgical treatment for the ear drum injury he experienced while in Greenwood. Even though my brother and I were in the same school, I did not see him during the day. I did manage to get into the junior high band playing the drums and cymbals again. It was fun and prepared me for a great tenth grade year with the high school marching band. I had a very dynamic teacher for algebra and science. She was very committed about preparing us to become college students. The foundation for my college career was laid there with Mrs. Kitchen.

One afternoon, I was out in our front yard and I heard a motor bike coming down the road. I looked up and thought it was someone I knew and I walked to the edge of the road. Sure enough it was Butch Daily, a boy that also played in the percussion section of the band. I was surprised he lived in the community. He did not ride the school bus nor did he go to the church we attended. We had many good times in the band as Butch had much natural talent and he was always trying to teach me something new. One day, Butch just quit showing up.

After about a week, the band director made an announcement that Butch had leukemia and was not expected to live. I saw his drum sticks on a shelf in the percussion section. I took the sticks and thought I would take them to him. It took me a few days to search out exactly where he lived and I asked my Dad to take me to his house so I could give him his drum sticks. Butch died the next day and I never got to see him. I did find out that his Mom worked in the library I frequented in the afternoons. I gave the drum sticks to one of the librarians who frequently assisted me and told her what they were and she promised to give them to Butch's Mom.

So here I was, getting close to finishing the ninth grade, with a heavy hearted feeling about leaving Greenwood and the fellowship of the Harris community. Ma and Pa had both died in our home while at Harris. We came to Anderson and Poochie died. Now a schoolmate had died. No one knew of the emotional woundedness I was experiencing. The night time awakenings slowed up and when they did happen, I learned that it may hurt in the right now, but it would be better by morning. I never had any awareness that any of my friends had those kinds of hurts. I always tried to follow the teachings of Sunday School teachers and do well in school work because I believed what my Dad told me about good school grades getting me into college and having a better life.

Even though Mrs. Franklin was helping Mom become more reality bound, Mom was getting restless because she had no other positive relationships in the church or in the neighborhood with anyone else. Mom started talking to Dad about trying to find a house closer to his office and perhaps we could go to the church on the Orr Mill Village. Maybe it would be like Harris since it was a village church. By the time school was out, Dad had found a place on East River Street closer to town and two miles from Orr Mill and church. We were on the move again.

CHAPTER TEN

EAST RIVER STREET

THE MOVE TO EAST RIVER Street was between my ninth and tenth grades. The house was in a grove of large pecan trees. The trees provided much shade to keep things cool in the warm months. The house had six large rooms. My brother finally did get his own bedroom. We rented from a lady who lived up the hill from us in a large two-story home with tall columns in the front, looking much like the way old plantation homes were described in books. We were allowed to gather all of the pecans and take them to the market with the money being ours. My brother and I made four to five dollars a week for several weeks.

We started attending the Orrville Baptist Church on the Orr Mill Village. Most of the members lived on the village or worked in the mill and lived nearby. Mom began to feel at home and started working with the GAs again. My brother, sister, and I all fell in love with the choir and activities for our age groups. My Dad worked with the RA boys' baseball team. To my utter surprise and amazement, my Sunday School teacher ended up being Mrs. Kitchen, my ninth grade math and science teacher. She was so dynamic and taught me survival skills for the rest of my life.

Mrs. Kitchen used much drama each week to have us look at our hands and wiggle each finger. Then we had to hold our ears and realize we could hear. We would move our legs to verify we could walk. We had to say "Jesus Loves Me" when we looked at her. When we completed the exercise, she would pronounce we had a mind that could think and work. Then, came the big, therefore. Because all of our parts were working well, our God compels us to develop them to the best of our ability for the purpose of serving Him and others. If we failed to do so, it was sin because we would be showing ingratitude for all that God had given us. Her mantra still comes to mind every time I am at a crossroad or making a decision about my life and living.

Entering the tenth grade meant attending the Anderson Girls' High School, also known as TL Hanna High. I think at that time Anderson was the only district in South Carolina that separated boys and girls in high school. Since we now lived in town, there was no school bus to pick us up in the mornings. I was expected to pay to ride the city bus. My brother and sister were in walking distance to their schools. Dad carried me to school in the mornings on his way to work. The city bus ride home was an adventure every day, with more disgusting adventures than good ones. At times, it was frightening. Finally, I figured out that I could ride the school bus down to the junior high school and just walk on home from there.

At eleven o'clock every school day, a bus picked up the girls in the band at the girls' high school. The band members from the boys' high school were picked up on a separate bus. The girls and boys were transported to the band room on the property of the McCants Junior

High Scholl located across the alley from the football stadium. We were outfitted and prepared to march in all of the football games. Sometimes there were extra practices in the afternoons. Buses transported us to the out of town games. I was also in the pep band which played on the town square every Thursday evening for the pep rallies during football season.

The band also became a mail service between the boys' and girls' high schools. The girls would write notes to their boyfriends at the boys' school and pass them on to a band member that would exchange them with band members from the boys' school who would deliver them to classmates on return to the school after band practice. The girls in the band also carried back to the girls' school, the notes from the boys to their girlfriends. When we returned to the school after band practice, it was lunch period for the school and everyone was waiting to see if their name was called to receive a note.

A special experience for the band each year was being invited to march at a Clemson football game. Local high school bands were invited to join together for part of the half time activities. We would go in early in the morning and practice with the other schools for the half time activity in the afternoons. Going to the Clemson ballgames was cost prohibitive for our family so it impressed the family that I got to go up to Clemson for a football game.

I did start dating some in the tenth grade and it drew forth yet another variant in behavior from my Mom. Mom was aware of the note writing between the girls' and boys' high schools. She was inquisitive about any notes I may have received. One day, Mom asked me about something that she could not have found out about unless she had read one of the notes in my pocketbook. I wanted to verify her deeds so I deliberately planted seeds about some things that might be on the sly regarding a church social for high schoolers. When I went to bed, I placed my purse near the bed and just pretended to be asleep. Sure enough, when she thought I was asleep she tiptoed in and removed my pocket book from the table. When she got to the doorway, I sat up in bed and asked her why she would come sneak off with my purse. She threw the purse at me and to my knowledge, she never did that again.

I was not around during my sister's teenage years but I have wondered at times if Mom treated her the same way as she treated me during her teen years. Mom wanted to know everything I did when it came to dating. All I know is that my sister did experience some difficulties during her high school days and even dropped out for a while. She finally graduated from high school. Whatever did happen with my sister, it was such that she denies having any memory of those years except for remembering the addresses of the places she lived. My brother has a little more memory about his teenage years but few specifics. I have been able to stimulate him every now and then for a few details.

The house on River Street was very roomy with a long wide hallway. It was not like other places we had lived where in any part of the house, you could hear what was going on all over the house. At the house on River Street, you could not hear if someone was approaching the room where you were. One day I was nearing the kitchen and I overheard my Mom tell my brother that he was her favorite child. I was surprised because she had been telling me that for several years. It had always been a mystery to me, for if I was her favorite, why did she treat me like she did? Why would you beat your favorite child?

My siblings received spankings, not beatings. Shortly after that surprise, I also overheard Mom tell my sister the same thing.

After about five months at River Street, Mom noticed our landlord who lived in the big two story house up above us staring down at us from an upstairs window in her home. Our windows were only partially covered. Mom was highly agitated about the peering and began to find ways to completely cover all of the windows on that side of the house. We could not afford blinds or shades because the windows were oversized. However, we scavenged the cloth shops and found heavy fabrics and made curtains that were kept closed so no one could see inside. That frenzy with the sewing machine got me back into my sewing again. Mom was a good seamstress and together we made some beautiful church and school clothes. I mastered the skill of selecting a pattern and following the step by step instructions and Mom knew all of the improvisations in the craft of sewing. This was the time I learned how to make buttonholes, do zippers, and make the belt and the buckle.

Mom had settled in at the church and was satisfied with the friends she had made. Orrville church was a big supporter of the Connie Maxwell Orphanage. It was a real joy for some of the Orrville folk to have a former Connie Maxwell orphan as a member of their church. As usual, Mom got many miles out of her story about her attempt to run away from the orphanage. Dad was doing well in his job and always worked to keep the peace in our home. Mom could not let go of our nosey landlord and started her, "I think we just need to move closer to the church campaign." One of her lady friends, Mrs. Mayfield, at the church started keeping an eye out for a house that might be suitable for us.

It wasn't long before Mrs. Mayfield informed my Mom and Dad of a house across from hers that would be coming up for sale. The house was about three blocks from Orr Mill village and the church. The house also had a vacant lot on one side of the house and it went with the house. The Mayfields had an only child, a son, the age of my brother. It was felt the vacant lot would be a good place where the boys could keep neighborhood ball going year round. Being that close to the Orr Mill also meant we had easy access to the Orr Mill swimming pool. Not every mill village had a swimming pool.

The Mayfields both worked at Orr Mill, but as I look back on it all it was almost as though Mrs. Mayfield served as a real estate broker for my Dad to be able to buy the house. A man who ran an insurance office a few blocks away evidently financed the house because that is where my Dad would go to make payments every month.

So here we go again. We moved to Ashley Avenue in late Spring of my tenth grade.

CHAPTER ELEVEN

ASHLEY AVENUE

BEING ABLE TO OWN A home again seemed to bring a level of quiet comfort to my Dad. After all, he had come from doing payroll for a single mill, the Harris plant in Greenwood, to now doing payroll for all of the mills in the Lowenstein Company. He was a hard worker and had a steadiness to keep on, even when faced with the challenges my Mom created for the family. My Mom glowed in her new status as a home owner even though her baggage followed her.

Mom's baggage included maintaining a formal living room and dining room even at the expense of my brother not having a bedroom again. The middle room in the back of the house should have been his bedroom but as before, he had a cot sort of bed, which doubled as a sofa in the television room.

The Ashley Avenue house had no air conditioning, but we did get a washing machine while there. The vacant lot next door turned into weekend ball games for the neighborhood. We had wonderful neighbors. The Mayfields, who helped my Dad seal the deal for the house on Ashley, were in front of us. The Pettigrews were on the side of us. Mrs. Mayfield and Mom shared sewing and cooking adventures. The Pettigrews had a modest home and Mr. Pettigrew was an outstanding gardener. His yard looked like one that could be on a magazine cover.

My Dad thoroughly enjoyed Mr. Pettigrew's advice on how to maintain our yard. Mr. Pettigrew was always sharing the seedlings that came up around his beautiful ornamental scrubs. Before the cold weather set in, we also had beautiful shrubbery beds, green grass, and all of our borders were lined with red crepe myrtle trees. Mr. Pettigrew became a good friend of my Dad. However, Dad carried a silent but heavy heart for Mr. Pettigrew. Mr. Pettigrew just would not attend church. His wife, Irene Pettigrew, was a faithful servant in our church. She also carried a heavy heart about the situation. Their boys had a non-serious attitude about church since their father did not attend.

Before we were ready, it was time to start school again. I entered the eleventh grade at the new girls' TL Hannah High School which was a good way from us, but I did have full school bus service from Ashley Avenue to the school. The following year the boys' high school was closed and the new girls' school became the new TL Hannah Co-ed High School of Anderson. My brother entered the ninth grade at the same junior high school where he had attended the seventh and eighth grades. My sister's "new school every year" journey continued.

As school started back, the youth choir also started back at church. I did not attend choir when we lived on River Street because of transportation issues. I was late for the first practice. When I walked in, a guy in the choir was staring me down. He was sitting next to one of the guys I knew from the band. After choir practice, the guy I knew from the band introduced me to his cousin, Mike.

Mike was a football player for the high school team, the Anderson Yellow Jackets, and a rising senior.

One thing I had learned the year before, from being in the band, was that all of the football players and their dates attended a free dinner at the Shinning Tower Restaurant in North Anderson following the home games. Some of the girls in the band were always bragging about having a date with a football player after the game and the free food. Indeed, I did get an invitation for a date after the next home football game. It was awkward wearing the band uniform, but I was not the only one. That was the beginning of a two-year courtship.

While on Ashley Avenue, my Mom was constantly trying to hire me out to do jobs for folk. I was hired out to do ironing and clean houses. Then she finally got Mrs. Pettigrew next door to get me a Saturday job in town where she worked. It was a dress shop on the square. I made five dollars every Saturday. Mom was able to get my brother a job on Riverside Mill village, a few miles down the road, where he would collect the paper route every Friday afternoon and Saturday morning. Sometimes I would drive him around to do the collecting. He did not have to deliver the papers. I just never did figure out why Mom never worked to amount to anything.

In Greenwood, she had worked for a few weeks part-time as a clerk in a drug store but could not get along with the owner's wife who Mom went in to relieve in the afternoons. All of the other wives on the mill village worked in the mill. Mrs. Pettigrew also found Mom a part-time job at one of the stores downtown but it did not last long. Mom felt one of the fulltime clerks was out to get her.

While living on Ashley Avenue, I do not recall having company from my Dad's family or my Mom's sisters. Occasionally we would go to Greenwood to visit my aunt and uncle. If we had time, Dad would go by Harris and catch up with a few folks. Thanksgiving was uneventful. At church, we were already getting ready for the Christmas musical. At home, Dad had started up with his usual, singing Christmas songs and reading "Twas the Night Before Christmas." We got out the Christmas decorations and started working to locate the burned-out bulbs. If one light was out on the strand, every light had to be tested to locate the one not working. It took hours to work through the strands. I did get some extra hours at the dress shop during the Christmas season and had some money of my own to spend.

I had something special to do to get ready for Christmas. This was the first Christmas I needed to get a gift for the person I was dating. The information I picked up from schoolmates was that the girls were to give their boyfriends a special brand name shirt and it was expected that the guys would give the girls a sweater. I bought Mike the dress shirt I was hearing about and he gave me a beautiful aqua colored sweater. Aqua was my favorite color. He told me his Mom helped him pick it out. I made me a strait wool skirt to wear with the sweater. The wool was tweed with some aqua in it. Our family Christmas was mostly giving and receiving needed items. I received a pair of popular loafers called "weejuns" from Santa. I do not recall a big family meal that year with any of my Dad's family or my Mom's sisters.

Mike had grandparents on both sides of his family and several aunts, uncles, and cousins. I did go with him to several family meals on both sides of his family. I was definitely aware he had a type of family-ness I knew nothing about.

About a month after Christmas, I came home after school one day to find out from a neighbor lady that my Mom had been carried to the hospital earlier that day. She thought my Dad was on the way home and we would go back to the hospital together.

I guess my brother and sister stayed at the house with neighbors checking in on them. Dad did not have much to say on the drive back to the hospital. This was the first time I had gone to a hospital to visit anyone with unknown circumstances. We entered a large multiple story brick building and rode an elevator up. It was not long halls with many rooms opening up. It was short halls with large wards of beds. Going out the side of one ward would open into another ward of six to eight beds. After going through one ward, we finally got to my Mom. She was in the corner of an eight-bed ward. She was medicated and moaning heavily, almost in a resistive way. She seemed to know who we were but acted like she did not hear us. Her hands were very swollen. We did not stay long.

On the way home, I asked my Dad what happened. He said she had suddenly started having much pain in her bones. The next evening, I went back to the hospital with Dad. This time Mom was yelling for us to get her out of there. She was refusing her medications, saying the medication would make her crazy like her mother. Her knuckles were red and swollen and she said her shoulder was hurting, but she did not want any medication.

In two days, Mom was back at home. She was in constant pain but refused medications. This was the beginning of an unrelenting hate journey she had with the medical profession for the rest of her life. It did seem to be connected with what she had observed at the Georgia State Mental Hospital when she would visit her mother.

She did think that her mother would get better if she did not take the medication.

Following Mom's hospital saga, the buzz in my life became the high school prom. Mike had invited me and I had no idea how I would get a prom dress. I told Mom and she thought she and I together could make a suitable dress. There were different types of fabrics to purchase, patterns, and special petticoat material. I was still working at the dress shop and had the money. I had to buy long gloves that came above my elbow. When the big night came, I gave Mike a boutonniere to wear on his white jacket, and he brought me an orchid to wear on my wrist. With all of the ado about what to wear to the prom, it never dawned on me that the prom was about dancing. I knew nothing about dancing. We survived the evening as wall flowers. After the prom, our BTU leader had a post prom party at her house. I was glad when it was all over. The dress was heavy and hot.

Mike's family started inviting me over on Saturday evenings for their family meal. Mike's Dad always grilled out on Saturdays. As a skilled machinist, he had made his own special grill. I was totally caught off guard when every plate was served up with individual T-bone steak. Never had I had a piece of real steak, much less one that did not have to be shared. In our home, we did good to get a small piece of cubed steak which was more flour and gravy than meat. Moreover, my family was concerned that I ate the whole steak. I became very aware that not all homes operated as ours. Mike's Mom and Dad both worked in the cotton mill. His Mom was a spinner and his Dad worked in the machine shop.

Shortly after the prom, our family was hit with a bombshell almost. Once again, we were going to have to relocate. This time was not about my Mom's unrest. Rather, it was a corporate transfer for my Dad. Life was good. Why now? Mom was settling down. Dad was enjoying coaching RA baseball. School was good for all of us. The Anderson site of the corporate offices was being relocated to Rock Hill, South Carolina. It was about a hundred miles from Anderson. This time the move was being paid for by the company. All we had to do was pack our belongings into boxes. Movers would come in and pick up everything, carry it all to Rock Hill, and unload it all. We did not have to be up there until the first of August.

Dad was able to finish up the season with the RA baseball team. They went out as winners in their league. My sister and one of her friends had served as batgirls. Mike's sister had served as score keeper. Dad had traveled up to Rock Hill and found a rental house for us. The Anderson house on Ashley Avenue sold in a timely manner.

It was hard for me to handle this with Mike. He had turned down a football scholarship to Presbyterian College to stay at home and attend Anderson College. And now, I would be in Rock Hill.

Leaving the church was hard on all of us. We had all settled in at Orrville Baptist Church and felt like it was home. Mom was doing well in the church. Her GA girls gave her a Bible when we left and she still had it when she passed away in 2015. We left Anderson in 1962. There was a new type of road most of the way to Rock Hill. It was a four-lane interstate highway. It made the trip easy. So, we are on the move again.

CHAPTER TWELVE

ARCH DRIVE TO MIDVALE AVENUE

SUMMER OF 1962 BECAME GLOOMIER every day for my brother, sister, and me. Knowing we would soon be in another school system by fall was a shared but silent sadness. My brother and I would be in the same high school, with him in the tenth grade and me in the twelfth grade. My sister would enter Sylvia Circle Elementary School which was near the 553 Arch Drive house. Mom struggled to find her own peace about the move. Dad reassured us that life could become better because he would be making more money.

The Lowenstein Company had their largest operation in Rock Hill. It was a printing and finishing company. All of the fabrics produced in the cotton mills were sent to the finishing plant to be dyed and printed into marketable goods. God was continuing to use the cotton to bless our family with food, shelter, and clothing.

The rooms at the Arch Drive house were smaller but my brother did get his own small room with a bed and chest only. When the movers brought in the boxes labeled "kitchen," we were surprised to find most of the glassware and dishes broken. I guess in all of our other moves, with us doing the transport, we took more care in how the cartons were handled. This was a first. We had very few dishes and plates to eat from. Before that problem was solved, Mike called and he and his cousin wanted to come up for a Sunday afternoon. Mom decided we needed some dishes since company was coming.

Mom came up with some money and wanted me to go to town and buy dishes. It was about a ten block walk to the Woolworth's Dime Store on Main Street. She gave me a specific amount of money to spend on dishes and a dollar to keep in my pocket to get a taxi ride home since the dishes would be too heavy for the walk home. I bought two boxes with a service for four in each box, and some glasses. The clerk packed them for me and called a taxi to meet me at the back door. Mission accomplished. We now had dishes for our expected company.

Mike's visit to Rock Hill was one of many over the next school year. When he came, we would go over to the Glencarin Gardens. Glencarin Gardens was home to a botanical garden with fountains, bridges, grassy areas, trees, flowers, walking paths, and benches. Mike and I would sit for hours and discuss his days as a freshman at Anderson College and my senior year at Rock Hill High School. We always ate at the house. This was the year I learned to make pizza from the box.

When we were living on Ashley Avenue in Anderson, I began to sense that feeling of community I knew so well when living on the mill village at Harris. We were near the Orr Mill and we attended the Orrville Baptist Church. Here in Rock Hill, I could tell there would be no sense of community again. We did not live near a mill nor was there a village church. It would be over fifty years before I ever had that sense of community again. We ended up joining the First Baptist

Church of Rock Hill. Needless to say, we were misfits in the First Baptist Church culture of anywhere. However, it did give my Mom a feeling of status. I did not get involved in any of the activities at church other than attendance on Sunday morning and Sunday evenings.

There was one girl, Roberta, in my girls' Sunday School class who seemed to be a loyal friend over the years but we did not actively stay in touch except near reunion times. We did not run into each other during the school day. As our parents aged, we were aware of the status changes in their health. In our co-ed Sunday School Department, there was a young man, Paul Campbell, who had much to do with a direction my life took after high school.

At school, I came to know three girls right well. One sat behind me in homeroom and introduced me to her friends. I was refreshed when one of the girls, Veda, attended the funerals of my parents. They tried to get me to join the band at Rock Hill High when they learned I had been in the Anderson band, but I chose not to take on the band as a senior and the new kid on the block. My studies went well and I had two teachers that implanted life lessons within me that continued to keep giving over the years. Mrs. Good embedded the craft of writing, both style and content. Mrs. Jolly taught psychology. As I look back on it, I think she knew she had students who were going through tough issues that they did not understand as a twelfth grader. She encouraged us to be patient and realize it could be ten years or more before we came to name and label all of the dynamics in our situations, but we would understand it better when we were older.

For me it was so true. When things got crazy at home with Mom, I was comforted to know it may not make sense now but one day I would be able to put the parts together. Among other issues, I did have a few of those recurring horrible sobbing episodes during the night while living on Arch Drive. I would wake up thinking about my grandmother who had passed away in our home when I was in the sixth grade. I did apply what Mrs. Jolly taught about not understanding the hard time now but one day I would understand.

My senior year came and went with very little drama. We just did not have the money for me to participate in many activities. I did not even think about going to the prom. Mike was a freshman at Anderson College. He and some of my brother's friends would come up at least once a month. Likewise, my brother and I would go back to Anderson about once a month also. My classmates were talking about going to college. I did not see it as a viable option for me even though I did have good grades. Near the end of my senior year, my Mom started going around town trying to find me a job. She got the manager of a new dime store to talk to me and he did offer me a part-time job until school was out and then it was to become fulltime.

Around the same time, my Dad bought a house at 816 Midvale Avenue about a mile from the Arch Drive house. The first thing he did was have a large window unit air conditioner installed. It was our first place to live with air conditioning. The house was a slight upgrade in neighborhood, small but adequate.

Back in Anderson, as Mike finished his freshman year at Anderson College, he decided not to continue. He had taken a job driving an ambulance and was contemplating joining the Air Force. He made his decision around the first of July to enlist in the USAF. Then he went home and told his parents after he had signed the paperwork. They took it hard. He was scheduled to depart from Charlotte, North

Carolina, for basic training at Lackland Air Force Base in San Antonio, Texas, near the end of the month.

I had some realization that my life was beginning to change. I felt like I needed to do more with my own life. I secretly began to explore the cost of attending Winthrop College as a day student. It seemed like something I could afford. I was giving my Dad most of the money I made on my job and he was keeping it for me. The Sunday following my finding out that the cost was very low for a day student, we had an unexpected speaker in our Sunday School Department. It was Paul Campbell, a member of the department and also a recent high school graduate. Paul gave a moving testimony about how he was changing up the expected career path he was on to a more specific path he felt the Lord was laying on his heart. And it was not full-time ministry, just a change up in the secular world.

Upon hearing what Paul had to say, I was called to reflect on what Mrs. Kitchen had taught us in Anderson about using all that God had given us. I knew that morning I had to go to college and that I would go home and talk with my folks. I told them at lunch, and also told them what it would cost. Dad said I had that much money saved and opened his wallet and showed it to me. Of course, Mom reminded me I could still work. The next week was demanding with time being so short and many details to work out before school started.

On Monday, I went over to Winthrop and got the particulars settled for admission and a schedule. The plan became that Dad would drop me off at Winthrop in the mornings. I would be finished with classes by noon, and have time to walk to the parking lot at his office by his lunch hour at one o'clock. I would carry my lunch and he would drop me off at the store where I worked.

The walk from the back side of the Winthrop campus to get to the parking lot where my Dad's car was parked turned into an education of its own. Upon leaving the back side of the campus, I started approaching the properties of the printing and finishing plant. I would walk to West White Street, turn left and walk up a long sidewalk to get to his car. There were six very large buildings actually covering over twenty acres. Each building seemed different. I started asking Dad about what went on in each of the buildings. Little by little I learned about the entire process of what happened when the cotton left the cotton mill as raw cloth or fabric from the loom. In the industry, the raw fabric was called gray goods. More professionally it was known as greige goods.

The gray goods that left Orr Mill in Anderson were transported to the printing and finishing plant, also called the bleachery. The finished cloth left the plant and made its way to sewing halls where it was turned into sheets and other cotton goods for consumption in the market place.

All of this was going on while I was getting used to Mike being out in Texas. We were exchanging letters every day and missing each other. He expected to get his permanent orders by end of September at the end of basic training.

The school routine was becoming a struggle to get there, get to work, and get home every day. I had no quality time or space to study and was beginning to feel the pressure of not doing as well as expected.

Mike got his orders to go to Bunker Hill Air Force Base in Peru, Indiana. He would be coming back to South Carolina for a week before having to report in Indiana. I was looking forward to seeing him. The anticipation was keeping me a little more distracted from school work.

Mike flew back into Charlotte, North Carolina. I drove to the airport to pick him up. We went out to eat and he gave me a diamond and asked me to marry him. Wow! I was not expecting that. We went back to Midvale where Mike would be staying until his parents came to get him the next morning. I showed my folks the ring and it was a dud type of reaction because it was bedtime for them. The next morning, Mike's parents arrived and I showed them the ring. They were nice about it but I could tell they were not expecting to see a diamond ring either. Mike went back to Anderson for several days and returned to Rock Hill the morning he was to depart for Bunker Hill Air Force Base. As far as everyone understood, we were engaged to be married at some later date; I was going to college and Mike was stationed in Indiana.

It did not take much time for my Mom's wheels to start spinning about getting rid of me. Another family from Anderson, transferred to Rock Hill in the same company move with us, had a daughter near my age. She got pregnant and my Mom was involved in helping her Mom plan a quickie wedding to get Jane married and moved on out of town.

About a week later, my Mom started telling me she thought I was pregnant and that I needed to be married. She wanted Mike's phone number and the number of his parents. I was so shocked. I still did not fully understand the birds and bees but felt sure I had not been close enough to get pregnant. Making long distance phone calls was expensive back then and I felt she was very serious when she started making those calls. She was ugly to Mike's mother on the phone. I think my future mother-in-law was putting my Mom in her place. It was a horrible few days. Mom was totally out of control. It was the first time I had ever seen my Dad slowed down by anything. He laid on the sofa and we had to carry him cold cloths to put on his head. He could not manage my Mom's behavior.

I formally dropped out of Winthrop. I quit my job. I bought a white brocade tablecloth and made myself a white dress to wear for a wedding ceremony at the Bunker Hill Air Force Base Chapel to be performed by the base Chaplain. Then I was surprised. Since my Mom had convinced me I could be pregnant, it was a shock to start having my monthly period. Then she started instructing me on how to use condoms so I did not get pregnant.

Nonetheless, Mom and I loaded up on a Greyhound bus and headed to Indiana for a wedding. It was a very sad time for me. I did not understand what was happening. Everything seemed out of control. Mike was as supportive as he could be on the phone. After all, he had a bride coming. There was a deep, deep inner pain as Dad pulled out of the driveway taking Mom and me to the bus station. Mom did take a picture of Dad and me with my brother and sister on the front stoop before we got into the car. I still have a copy of that photo and can see by their faces they were in as much shock and disbelief as I was.

CHAPTER THIRTEEN

MARRIAGE IN INDIANA

SO HERE I AM ON a Greyhound bus with a mother who is not like the mothers of my friends. She had done things in the past, most of which the entire family helped to cover up. Unlike those physical beatings in the past, when I found a place to hide from her, this emotional whipping was far reaching. My strategy was to pretend to be sleeping so I would not have to talk to her. It also provided some quality time for thinking through all that was happening.

I considered that leaving to get married was my only option. It did give me a place to be received and wanted. If I had not followed through with the marriage, I would have left home with no place to go. Staying in the home with my Mom was no longer an option for me. As I laid my head back and pondered the events, my thoughts wandered to what Mrs. Jolley had said in school. Even though I did not understand it all right now, there would come a day when I would understand. Right now, I had to figure how to just live through it all.

The bus arrived in Peru, Indiana, midafternoon October 26, 1963. Mike had borrowed a car from a friend on base and picked us up. We went by the small three room apartment Mike had rented for us and dropped off most of what we had brought from Rock Hill. Mike also had some things to take in since he was in process of moving out of the military barracks. I had all of my clothes in two suitcases. Mom had brought two suitcases with household supplies including a pot and a pan, and some odd and end utensils. There were also a few dishes and linens. It was a shock to see the apartment above a grocery store where we had to share the bathroom with an adjoining apartment.

Then we headed out to the edge of town to a restaurant for supper. After supper, Mom and I checked into a motel next door to the restaurant. Mike went on back to the base. He was to pick us up in the morning for the trip out to the chapel on the base for the marriage.

We had breakfast at the restaurant. Mom paid for everything. I had never done so much eating out before. We went back to the room and I put on the white dress and got fixed up for my marriage. Mike was on time picking us up and off we went to Bunker Hill Air Force Base. The sight of so many military jets all around me was almost overwhelming. We made our way to the chapel and the Chaplain on duty met us and performed the ceremony after I signed a marriage license.

We drove back to Peru and checked out of the motel room and loaded the car. I did not get to change clothes and had to go into the restaurant for lunch in the white dress. I felt like people were staring at us. After lunch, we drove Mom back to the bus station where she caught a bus back to South Carolina. Yes, she was gone.

Mike and I drove to our apartment. Wow, we were husband and wife and all alone for the first time. It was awkward and I really found out about the close contact needed to make a baby. Actually, it was painful but Mom had told me it would get easier. We also spent time unpacking our things and trying to figure how we would live in such a small place and share a bathroom with strangers. The next morning, Mike drove his buddy's car back to the base. When he came home in the evening, he was dropped off by his Sargent who lived down the road. This would become Mike's means of transportation to and from the base until we could get a car. I started venturing out some during the day while Mike was gone. There was a real grocery store about a block and a half down the street. I learned the hard way not to buy more than you could carry if alone. When going up the street you crossed over the Wabash River and a small town opened up.

I enjoyed walking by the various businesses and seeing what was what. I did come upon a Spiegel Catalog Store. You could go in and look through the catalog and order items. After you ordered your first item, you could have your own catalog to take home. I became a big fan of Spiegel. The laundromat was located about three blocks from the apartment. We would put our soiled clothes in a duffel bag, and walk across the Wabash River to the laundry.

A few weeks after arriving in Peru, I noticed a "Help Wanted" sign in the window of the Bearss Hotel in town. They were looking for a daytime switchboard operator. I got the job and our income grew. Mike's parents had been generous to send us money for a television. When we purchased the television, we had to hire a cab to get home with it. We were able to get a telephone and would call home once per month and they would call in between our calls. Letter writing was almost a daily practice.

I inquired with folk where I worked about churches in the area and found out there was a small Southern Baptist Church about four blocks from the apartment. We started walking to church on Sundays. If it was raining, someone would pick us up. One day while walking to work, I noticed a "For Rent" sign pointing around a corner. I watched it for several days and one day on the way home from work, I walked to the house. The owner lived in front and had a small apartment in the back and it had a private bath. Mike looked at it the next day and we decided to move. The rent was a few dollars less.

Getting a private bathroom was important to us. Every time you used the shared bathroom, you had to scrub it down when you left it. One day I had sprinkled scouring powder in the tub. I got distracted and forgot to finish with scrubbing out the tub. Later that day, the gentleman we shared the bath with was entering the building as we were coming in. He apologized about not knowing it must be a Southern custom to leave bath powders in the tub after a bath. However, he had some and from now on would always be leaving bath powder in the tub after he used it. We got in and sure enough, Old Spice talcum powder was sprinkled in the tub.

We started carrying some things in suitcases to the new place until we got it down to what would fit into a taxi. We were able to save some money and Mike's parents sent us five hundred dollars. We finally had enough to make a down payment on a car. We bought a new 1964 Chevy Nova. Life changed for us greatly. We had more independence. We could now travel to places further than walking distance. I felt like we were moving up in the world because we moved to an even larger apartment with four rooms.

Back home in South Carolina, my brother, when getting his physical exam to play football, was discovered to have a heart murmur and was being sent to Emory Medical Center in Atlanta. I did not know how my family would handle the situation. I voluntarily sent them some money to help pay for the expenses. I was discussing the situation with the lady I worked for at the hotel and she thought I should go down to Rock Hill and travel with them to Emory. Mike agreed and we bought a ticket for me to ride the bus to Rock Hill.

The day after I arrived, we loaded up and headed to Atlanta. It was about a 250-mile trip so we left early and arrived for a mid-morning appointment. It was a somber trip. We all tried to talk about something funny which did not work. The silences were unbearable. There was so much unknown. As a family unit, we had been through much junky upheaval because of my Mom, but nothing had ever felt as life threatening as the possibility of heart surgery. When we would stop and go to the bathroom, my Mom always fussed at me for freshening my hair, face, and lipstick. On arrival at Emory, my brother was taken back for many tests and examinations by several doctors.

The outcome was that my brother could not play sports and they would reevaluate him in another month to determine if surgery was needed. He did have heart valve damage which was felt to be related to a severe case of measles he experienced while in grammar school. We headed back to Rock Hill. The ride home was long but much lighter. My Mom continued to fuss at me at every pit stop for using cosmetics.

The next day, I rode the bus back to Peru. I did notice when getting ready to leave that my cosmetics bag had disappeared. I was thankful I had the opportunity to be with my family during that ordeal, a husband who understood, and was appreciative to have a boss lady who encouraged me to go. When leaving to go to the bus station, I tried to give my Dad twenty dollars to help with expenses and he declined, saying I had already done enough. The next month was hard waiting out my brother's next visit to Emory. I did not go back to Rock Hill for the second visit. The next visit turned out about the same as the first one and my brother was to be followed by a doctor in Rock Hill. The damaged heart valve was replaced when he was sixty years old.

In the meantime, in Peru, the daughter of the pastor of our church worked as a nursing assistant at our local hospital. Since I now had transportation she asked me about coming to work at the hospital as a nursing assistant. It paid more than the switchboard job. I took the job for the money but soon learned the work was worthy and suited my personality. I grew up quickly as I cared for the sick and dying. Hospitals in the 1960s were just not anything like we know as hospitals today.

As I watched the registered nurses work, I realized that this was something I could do someday. I did experience two, deep emotional and life altering events while employed at the hospital. The first came after several weeks of caring for an older lady who was terminally ill. In all of my encounters with her, I felt like she was taking care of me. She was so kind, appreciative, and inspiring me to a spiritual way of thinking. As I look back on it all, I think she recognized my level of naivety and was preparing me for her passing.

After a few weeks, I was coming in for work and when the service elevator opened up for me, the undertaker was coming off with a body. And as it goes in hospital lingo I ask who, and he replied with the name of my patient and friend. All of a sudden, I knew all about heaven and that she was there. All of that sitting in church over the years never made it so real for me as that event in the elevator. I knew

I would miss her but I was joyful for her. My faith leaped. When I got up to the floor I went to the room she had occupied, I found it empty. However, my soul was at peace.

The second hospital event that spoke volumes to me was the night the ambulance brought in a young boy who was playing at the railroad tracks in an open boxcar. The train started to roll. The child jumped off and fell under the train and his legs were cut off. Our job was to stabilize him so he could make the transport to Indianapolis. After the child left our small facility, the chatter exploded about who the child was. People from town kept pouring in wanting details.

Peru had been the wintering grounds for the Ringling Brothers Circus for years. Even though the circus now wintered in Florida, many circus folk retired to Peru. The child who lost his legs was the son of a very famous circus person who still worked in his infamous role but not for the circus. The local story was sad about how the child would go to the train station everyday thinking this might just be the day his Dad would come in on the train. Over the next few weeks, the locals who had contact with what was going on in the Indianapolis hospital would come by the hospital and let us know what was going on with the child.

Finally, Mike had accrued enough leave time that we started planning a trip back home to South Carolina. Often I would think of what might be going on with my brother and sister, given the ups and downs of my Mom's behavior. I wanted to take something to them. I did not want them to be embarrassed to have friends over. Mom could cook well and I thought if they could fix up a nice table when folk came over it might impress guests. The Spiegel catalog had a set of nice china on sale and a few other table trimmings. I was pleased to have the money to take something to the home that might make life less embarrassing for my brother and sister when friends came over.

Mapping out the trip was quite an ordeal. Mike and I had never been on a 650-mile auto trip. Following a paper map and watching for highway signs wore us out before stopping to spend the night. I guess we were still tired when we started out in the morning because Mike fell asleep and ran off the road but was awakened when hitting a terra-cotta. There was mild car damage but we were okay and continued on. The impact caused a cup from the box of china in the back seat to bounce out. However, the cup was recovered with no damage.

We finally arrived in Rock Hill. The china was well received. I had discussed with my brother about what he would be doing since he would soon be graduating from high school. He was unsure about college because of his grades and lack of money. I told him about a guest preacher I had heard at the Rock Hill church before I left home. The guest talked about a small Baptist college that was willing to serve folk in his situation. I helped him get started with the process and the rest is history. He attended North Greenville Junior College and received the help he needed to graduate and move on to a four-year Baptist college with the same philosophy. Eventually, he earned a master's degree from Clemson University.

My sister had few friends and did not enjoy school. She was not open to much discussion with us. Mom was eager to feed us well while there and did not want us to go visit Mike's folk in Anderson. Dad was gracious and knew we should go see Mike's folk.

We stayed in Rock Hill for two days and went to Anderson for three days. Mike had a lot of family to visit. This was the first time we had seen any of them since getting married. They were very open and welcomed me into the family. They were like real family with no one pretending.

It was a long ride back to Indiana but we had much to talk about. The Vietnam war was raging. Most of the airmen who had come from basic training to Indiana with Mike had already shipped out. We had discussions about what I would do if he got orders to ship out. Where would I go to live? I did open up the possibility of going to nursing school because I could live at the hospital since hospital schools of nursing provided housing for nursing students.

As time moved on, my brother did well at college and we sent him twenty dollars per month for spending money. Every day Mike and I lived in fear, "this would be the day he got orders to ship out." The stress of it all pushed me to explore the nursing school at Charlotte Memorial Hospital, in Charlotte, North Carolina. The education office at the Air Force Base worked with the school of nursing and administered all of the admissions test to me. We were able to get everything set up for me to go to nursing school when Mike got shipped out.

Time moved on and Mike did not deploy. The days were getting short for me to enter nursing school. We assumed he would be getting deployed and I should go ahead and move down to the nursing residence at Charlotte Memorial Hospital in time to start. Mike moved into the barracks on base and I went on down to Charlotte.

When I look back on the days in Indiana, I can thank God for my mill hill heritage. I knew I had to work if I were to have anything. I knew how to cook and sew. I was blessed to be able to buy an electric sewing machine. I was able to make my clothes. The golf club on

Bunker Hill AFB was free to all airmen and their families. I took lessons and learned to play golf while in Indiana. Most of all I knew it all came by the hand of God and that I was to give thanks to Him. I was able to trust that His goodness would prevail.

I also had an awareness of the lack of a common, unifying mission of the local community in Peru, Indiana. Of course, there was the USAF base for the military residents. Most of the locals were detached from the base. In days gone by, there had been the pride of being the wintering grounds for the Ringling Brothers Circus, all of what was a fading memory. There were numerous very small churches, but no one major faith group.

The only crop that grew in the summers was corn. Huge corn fields were everywhere. Cotton was not the king crop and there were no snowy white fields in late summer. Cotton had provided the livelihood for both Mike's family and mine. Most of all, the strong spirit of the church, the unity and common mission of the mill hill culture shaped the early years of our marriage even if in Indiana.

CHAPTER FOURTEEN

NURSING SCHOOL, BIBLE COLLEGE, AND FAMILY

TRANSITIONING TO DORMITORY LIVING HAD its challenges. Forty females on one hallway with a communal bath facility was an adjustment. We also had two pay phone booths on the hallway. Cell phones did not exist and there was no television. The two-story student nurse residence was located behind the hospital across from the residence for the interns and resident physicians. The future doctors had small apartments. Classroom time was at the local community college facility a few miles from the hospital. This was the first-year for the associate degree program as opposed to the three-year hospital based diploma school. We had classroom time two days per week and clinical time at the hospital three days per week.

There were a few other students on the hall who were also married. They stayed at the dorm four nights a week and went home Friday until Monday mornings. We all adjusted well to the awkwardness of our situations. I was able to get a part-time job working on the hospital switchboard since I had experience from the hotel in Indiana. After about three months, it was apparent that Mike would not be shipping out. I went back to Indiana and spent Christmas break with him.

By late Spring, we were planning on his discharge and how we would manage our circumstances. Over the previous year or so, Mike had made a decision to attend Piedmont Bible College in Winston Salem, North Carolina, when discharged. One of the married girls in the dorm was from that part of North Carolina. Being able to commute back and forth with her was a God send.

Mike was able to secure a good part-time job while in school. One of Mike's family friends in Anderson was the purchasing agent for the cotton mill where the family worked. He knew a supplier that owned a business in Winston Salem and referred Mike to him. The job was literally waiting for Mike and synced well with his school schedule. Once again, we were blessed by the cotton. The part-time job along with his GI Bill provided adequate income. All expectation was that I would go to work as a registered nurse when I graduated.

As nursing school was nearing an end, I looked back at my most memorable experiences. The first unforgettable moment was in my first clinical rotation which was on the burn unit. I will never understand why they would start out a newbie on such a unit. It was harsh to the eyes and heart. I had a beautiful female patient who had severe burns to her torso and extremities. The second week I was there, she asked me to make arrangements for her husband to bring their daughter up to see her. She wanted to see her daughter one more time because she knew she would never get back home. The arrangements were made. They did come to see her the following day. When I reported for my next duty on the unit, I was told she had passed away a few hours after her husband and child had visited.

The second memorable thing to me was in my psychiatric nursing rotation. It was there that I began a long journey of learning about my mother's disposition. All of the childhood trauma she went through plus the fact that her mother suffered with manic depression (as it was called back then) gave rise to my Mom's erratic behaviors. This started a processing journey that has been with me ever since.

The third and more pleasant memory was on my pediatric rotation. Back in Indiana I had been on duty one night in the hospital when the young boy was brought in with legs amputated after he fell under the rolling train. I heard much about his famous father back then but never dreamed I would meet the child's father. When reporting to duty on the pediatric unit one morning, we were told that Emmet Kelly Jr., the now famous Kodak clown, still a mime, would be on the unit for pictures with the children.

Wow! When I entered a patient's room there he was! Emmett Kelly Jr., and the Kodak cameramen were on the far side of the room with the child next to the window. As he completed his visit with that patient, he came to the bedside where I was working. After the picture was taken of him with my patient he prepared to leave the room. As he was leaving, I told him I knew he could not speak but I wanted him to know I was with his son the night he was brought to the emergency room, that horrible night in Peru, Indiana. He stood still and stared at me with increased moisture in his eyes.

Later that day, down in the hospital lunchroom, the Kodak folk and Emmett Kelly Jr. were working the room taking group pictures with employees. We did make eye contact as I went through the food line and at times when I was near to where he was posing with groups. Several days later, in my hospital mailbox, I had an envelope with no address or name. I opened the envelope and there were several pictures of me with or near Emmett Kelly Jr. What a surprise! There was no mistake that he knew what I was saying to him and that the event of his son losing his legs was emotional for him. I asked around and was told that I was the only staff person to get individual pictures with Emmett Kelly Jr. The rest were group pictures or department pictures. I told them I had helped take care of his child several years earlier. It did make folk wonder. It was obvious that he must have told one of the photographers to get a few shots of me when near him.

The summer that I was completing nursing school, Mike went back to Orrville Baptist Church in Anderson to assist his former pastor, Dr. Clarence Martin. I would go down on the weekends.

Graduation happened. I was happy to shed those navy-blue student uniforms and white aprons to wear a full white uniform, white hat, white stockings, and white shoes. Another good thing, besides no more commuting, I was pregnant when I graduated. It was a pleasant surprise. I did go to work for about four months before our son was born.

Our families were delighted to hear about the pregnancy. Our church in Winston Salem had a group of middle aged women who felt it a ministry to work with younger women with first time pregnancy. We had much love and support around us.

This was a very special time for us. Besides the pregnancy, it was the first time in our marriage that I felt we were in an environment similar to how we were raised. Indeed, there is power among the fellowship of believers. Even though Mike was in school, we had a normal routine. He went to school in the mornings and worked in the afternoons. We had an adequate income for prudent living.

On weekends, we often visited our families in Rock Hill and Anderson. Mike had a large, endearing, and open family on both his Mom and Dad's side. They embraced me with much love. My family was very different. My Mom had her sisters who all lived in the Atlanta area. They all carried their childhood baggage in various ways. Mom thought she was better than her sisters because she was not divorced. My Dad's family was small but warm and open with all of their warts.

My Dad continued to be the stabilizing force in my family of origin. Even though I had been away for a few years, my Mom continued to build fires that Dad had to put out. It was good for my brother that he went off to college when he did. He was able to discover other ways for life and living than what he knew as the norm in his home. My sister, who lived in a different house and attended a different school every year until the ninth grade, was without a stable connection to anything. The disconnection played out over her entire life.

My Mom spent much time in trying to cover up the problems with my sister. The one good thing that my sister learned was from our father. She knew she had to work. Within our cotton mill heritage, the value of working was embedded. With her life of living out the consequences of bad decisions, she did find some worth in being able to hold a job.

CHAPTER FIFTEEN

AND THEN THERE WERE THREE

EVEN THOUGH 1969 IS BEST known for the first man on the moon event, the biggest event in our life was the birth of our son Deveron Shane Smith on January 25. I worked up until about three weeks before he was born. In those last few weeks, we struggled for a name, should we have a boy. A girl's name had already been settled on. In our young naivety, we wanted a name that was different since the last name was Smith. During the days of the name struggle, we watched a Western movie titled "Shane." The movie character, Shane, was a hero and the name was not common back then. With the middle name settled, we began the search for a first name that would be even more different. Then we saw it a few days later as we read the credits following a television program . . . Deveron.

Our families visited on a regular basis after Shane was born. Shane was the first grandchild in both of our families. My Mom was always telling me about how tired I was and how I would need some relief. Actually, I was feeling and doing just fine. I do not know how I would have been had I not gone through nursing school. It was nursing school that had prepared me for what to expect. In nursing school, I learned about both the emotional and physical care of self and others. After a month, I was beginning to think about how I would get back to work. The hospital was calling asking for a time frame for my return. A lady whose husband was in school with Mike agreed to come over in the afternoon and stay with Shane until Mike got home at five.

I returned to work when Shane was two months old. I worked the 3 pm to 11 pm shift three days per week. The work was intense and often without getting a supper break. This problem was fixable. I had noticed that many patients coming for surgery would hire private duty nurses to stay with them. To have just one patient for an entire shift sure seemed to be a better option for me. I went through the process to become eligible to get on the private duty roster. Back then, the private duty nurses had to be approved by the American Nurses Association unofficial local affiliate. This was before the days of intensive care units. I would call in and give them the days and hours I was available. When families put in a request for a nurse, they were informed about the cost and how to pay the nurse.

Private duty work gave me more control over my work environment, reducing the stress and fatigue level. I got to know some of the well-to-do families in Winston Salem. Often, they would call in advance of a need to schedule my services. Mike's work held firm with the company he was referred to from Anderson.

By mid-1970, Mike felt led to transfer to Bob Jones University in Greenville, South Carolina. At BJU, he could pursue the religious education track. We used Mike's Veteran's benefit to buy a small house in Greenville, located on 407 E. Hillcrest Drive. I was able to get a good job and we found a nearby Christian child care facility to help with care of our son.

To some, our life may have seemed hard and demanding, but to me it was freeing. I had learned from my growing-up that you had to work hard and get an education if you were ever to have anything. Mike had learned the same thing growing-up, but with less deprivation and more stability in his home life.

What could have been despair and gloom of my younger years was overshadowed by the light of the goodness of God. I can look back now and thank God for the light was always there as expressed by those He strategically placed around me and then, one day within me. I was never alone. And yes, I thank God for my mother because she brought me into this world. I was always aware of my reality but my unexpressed wounds walked beside me—not in front of me. The light was always there in the darkest of times.

Mike's family embraced me and filled many of the gaps in my life. Life was good. Two years after moving to Greenville, we were able to build a house about twelve miles from Greenville, in rural Lyman, 180 Brookdale Acres Drive. We remain in the same home today. However, we did live in the lower part of the state for several years as Mike served as a bi-vocational pastor. We were blessed to keep the Lyman home rented out while away.

So much of what I enjoyed in Mike's family I wanted to duplicate and make a part of our son's family of origin. We worked hard to try to make holidays meaningful events with my family, but commotion persisted no matter how hard we worked at it. I would start early to get them to commit for holiday meals and gatherings. When they would come, it was always awkward. My mother was never comfortable. However, they would meet us halfway anytime Shane could come spend time with them. We would meet at Stuckey's in Blacksburg and do the drop off/pick up. Shane enjoyed going to Rock Hill because there was a boy, Koby, next door to my parents who was Shane's age. The two boys shared backyard adventures for years. When Shane was in high school, Koby committed suicide. That event took eons to digest.

Our son remained an only child after several miscarriages. Shane enjoyed a quality school life, little league ball teams, and one year of high school football. Mike would help with coaching and my Dad would coach Mike on how to coach baseball.

Mother's Day May 16, 1976, was such a beautiful day in so many ways. Shane and I spent the morning in Rock Hill with Mema and Papa Tip. Mike had to work that day. For several months, especially when driving, Shane and I had been talking about his letting Jesus come into his heart. He said he had accepted Christ in Little Church one morning when Preacher Long brought a special message to the children. Shane knew Christ was in his heart but was afraid to be baptized. He thought Preacher Long might drop him in the water.

The week before Mother's Day, we were having a revival in our church with Ein Walker and Steve Taylor as guests. This week the talks with Shane became more serious and increasingly intense regarding his salvation. He seemed to be more aware that he must follow through with baptism. I never encouraged or discouraged. He would just talk on and on with me and I could tell he was getting it together and working it out for himself.

While driving to Rock Hill on Mother's Day morning, Shane and I did have an interesting conversation. He wanted to know about our bodies in heaven. What we would be like? Would we still have on the clothes we were buried in? He also spoke of seeing my Uncle Fred when we got to heaven.

The drive back to Lyman after lunch was pleasant. Mike was home when we got there and I informed him about the conversations with Shane and the passion in which Shane spoke. I was supposed to stay in the nursery that evening at church but was not needed when I checked in so I went and joined Mike and Shane in the worship service. It was a simple, thought provoking sermon. The invitation began and Shane told us he was ready to be baptized and had to go talk with the pastor. We tried to accompany him and he arrogantly announced for us to stay behind, "I'm doing it by myself."

And to make the day, we returned home to find our only gardenia bloom had opened and the fragrance was all about. Shane and I had been fussing and praying over that gardenia for days. It seemed the buds would just die and drop off before opening. We called Mema and Papa Tip and gave them the good news.

Indeed, we had a wonderful Spring in 1976. Shane had won the first-grade Bicentennial Costume Contest. Mema had made him a George Washington outfit. As the winner of the contest, he rode the school's float in the town's parade. He thought that day was more special than Christmas. He could not sleep the night before. After the parade, all of the festivities for such a small town as Duncan were far more than expected. There was a reenactment of the Battle of Fort Prince, along with booths demonstrating life in 1776. We bought fresh bread and watched quilting demonstrations, and many more. We were joined by Shane's uncle, Mema, and Papa Tip.

My Dad appreciated our trying to bring the family together for holidays because we always included his siblings, Ruth and Fred. Their wandering sibling, Ruby, showed up in the late 1980s after her husband in Virginia had passed away. She had many physical needs and nursing home placement soon became her best option. She did have the funds. With my local contact in the healthcare field we were able to get Ruby placed into a local facility. This took a load off my Dad because Mom had no use for Dad's family.

I frequently had questions of my Dad about the history of his family. I wanted to know more about them. I felt something was missing in my life since so many of Mike's family were in my face, both the living and all of the cemeteries where the dead were buried. Finally, my Dad gave in and decided we would go up to Fannin County, Georgia, where he still had some cousins. We went to Big Creek Church community. While walking in the church cemetery, someone came up who happened to be my Dad's cousin, Gober, who lived behind the cemetery. He was as tickled to meet us as we were to meet him.

Gober told us the story of Pa leaving the mountains of Fannin County, Georgia. Since Pa had a wagon and two mules, he got into the logging business near Candler, NC. He remembered Fred coming up there and filled in many of the gaps my Dad had in his memories as told to him by his father. To the side of Gober's dwelling was the remains of the old Tipton home place. A partial stone threshold and chimney were still standing. We recovered one of the stones, brought it home, had it engraved and have it to this day. The Big Creek Church was in the center of former moonshine territory. Moonshine was illegal liquor and the business of moonshining thrived in the days of prohibition. Gober rode with us and showed us the history of the liquor stills in the area. There were many stories about escaping the "revenuers." For several years, we visited the church on the first Sunday in August, known as Decoration Day in those parts. All graves in the church cemeteries were decorated that day along with picnic on the grounds and gospel music. We had never heard the song "Grace Was Found from the Saddle to the Ground" before, but it forever remained with us. Over the years, we had many conversations about the song and how very special it seemed to be to the folk in the Big Creek Church community. The song is about a bad guy riding on his horse when the horse became spooked. The bad guy was thrown to the ground and died. Sometime later folk were standing by his grave talking about how bad he was. Then flowers were noticed on the grave where God had written with the flowers, "Grace was found from the saddle to the ground."[4]

On another occasion, my Dad took us back to the area where his mother was from, near Candler, NC. These trips to visit the past did not set well with my Mom. She did not like to think about anything in the past or family connectedness. My mother also convinced both my brother and sister that thinking about the past was foolish. My brother and sister both married someone with disrupted pasts. I can look back on it now and see their struggle with abandonment issues. Therefore, our involvement with family roots was an uncomfortable conversation for them.

---

4 The Marksmen Quartet, vocal performance of "Saddle to the Ground," author unknown. Recorded on CD, In Performance, n.d. Donald J Shockey, vocal performance of *Grace Was Found From the Saddle to the Ground,* writer unknown, n.d. https://www.youtube.com/watch?v=IYKI6PC3TTY.

My Dad often joked with me over the issue of how hard he had worked to help his children have opportunities that would keep them from having to live a life dependent on the cotton mills. He considered himself to be the first generation uninvolved in moonshine liquor. His children were to be the first generation uninvolved with the cotton mills. When I went to work as the nurse for a cotton mill in Greer, South Carolina, he just never did fully adjust to the idea. I frequently humored him with the fact that I was there to help the mill workers, and that we did not live on the village.

To this day our son thanks God for my time working at the cotton mill in Greer. While there, I was able to trade my set of Gene Sarazen golf clubs with the plant manager for a pair of season tickets to Clemson football games. Clemson football has remained one of our family traditions ever since.

It is easy to sit back now and see how God was overshadowing my life. After all, I did go to church every week and was actively involved in church ministries. However, I was more attentive to having a good paying job so that we could have all of the right things. I did feel mightily blessed because we had "stuff." Little did I understand about how to live wholly, radically, dependent on the Triune God of this universe. Real life lessons were yet to come.

While our son, Shane, was growing up, we would occasionally see cotton growing in our area. Much of the cotton harvest was gathered by machinery then. On rare occasions, our son did see multitudes of folk in the cotton fields with those long bags on their back picking the cotton. There just were not as many cotton fields anymore. Whenever we did see a cotton field, I would tell him the stories of what I had seen while growing up, along with the stories from his grandparents about picking cotton.

While Shane was in his junior year of college, we lost Mike's mother very unexpectedly. The event drew forth a new pondering about the pain of grief and loss. There had been several deaths in Mike's extended family over the years. With this loss, things just did not return to normal like they had in the past. I did learn some lessons from the way Mike's family handled funerals. The funerals were organized with appropriate music and a special sort of funeral etiquette. Our son knew more about acceptable funeral practices than most young adults. He and his cousins from Anderson usually did quartet singing at the funerals in Anderson.

By the time Shane was finishing college, I too had been able to go back to school part time. I completed two more years, earning a Bachelor's Degree in Nursing. The objective had been to be able to make more money. However, that was not the case. I had maxed out the pay grade for my level in public health work. The entry level of pay in the next higher pay grade which required the Bachelor's Degree was lower than what I had been earning. That was hard to swallow. After living with that disappointment for a few months, I made the decision to pursue graduate school.

At the same time our son was finishing college, and we both experienced taking the Graduate Record Exam (GRE) together. As expected, he scored higher than I did but I met the requirement for full student status—no probation. However, Shane did not pursue graduate school. He had a very good job offer with an oil company in Louisiana. The company paid for a visit to the area to find a place to live and also the move from South Carolina to Louisiana. That may seem common place today but in our limited life it seemed like over the top good news.

I traveled to Louisiana with our son to help him find an apartment. We secured an apartment, and visited a church which he did later join, the First Baptist Church of Lafayette. The date was set for the movers to come. From our home, he carried his bedroom furniture, his piano, and other odds and ends. Mike and I were going to accompany him on the journey. However, my Mom insisted it would be too traumatic for us to drive off and leave our son down there. She insisted she and my Dad should be the ones to accompany Shane.

The following months were an adjustment. Shane did come home for the holidays and we visited him for special events. Mike would go down for golf tournaments and special men things. The culture was very different from anything we had experienced. He was located in the heart of Cajun country. Never had we been in an area where the protestant church did not prevail in culture and daily practices. Shane did sing in his church choir and we were blessed to attend one of their Christmas musicals.

The transition into the empty nest was met with ineffective coping, as I look back on it all. We filled our time with more church work and time-demanding jobs. I entered graduate school at Clemson. We also entered a season of coming alongside Mike's Dad as his health began to deteriorate. Our marriage was good and we had fun. We thought what was missing was our son. Little did we know.

There were few with whom we could discuss our true feelings even if we had been able to identify our feelings. Our day to day reality was changing. We assumed we were coping well with the empty nest through our busyness. We took my Dad's forever advice to just keep on keeping on.

Little did we understand about folk outside our small rural area of upstate South Carolina. For us, folk either went to church or they did not go to church. There seemed to be a knowing among those that did not go to church that there was a creator God and they were choosing not to follow the rules.

nest through our business. We took my Dad's forever advice to just keep on keeping on.

Little did we understand about folk outside our small rural area of upstate South Carolina. For us, folk either went to church or they did not go to church. There seemed to be a knowing among those that did not go to church that there was a caring God and they were choosing not to follow the rules.

CHAPTER SIXTEEN

THE EMPTY NEST BECOMES TOXIC

OUR SUNDAY SCHOOL CLASS HAD a special Labor Day tradition. We had a member, Mr. Neimi, who had a large farm. He was also a retired engineer. Mr. Neimi had built a miniature railroad track through some of his property with train cars capable of riding a dozen or so folk at a time. There was wide open pasture land and wooded trails for walking. Every Labor Day, Mr. Neimi hosted a major family event for all class members, their families, and guests. The major outdoor event was never rained out. It was a day to come relax with friends on the farm.

Shane flew home for the Labor Day weekend looking forward to the event and catching up with old friends. We had a photographer in our group who was always catching the moments for families. She enjoyed giving the photos to families. I always felt she did this because she and her husband rarely had visits from their adult children. The next day, we drove Shane to the airport for his trip back to Louisiana. On the way home from the airport, Mike asked me if I thought Shane was okay. We were in agreement that he did seem to be preoccupied. The next week at Sunday School our photographer friend gave us, not the usual three to four family pictures, but an album of numerous candid shots of the three of us interacting with one another and others. The photos did reveal that our son appeared more mature.

A few weeks later we traveled down to Shane's and carried a few items since he was relocating to a newly purchased home. Shortly after getting there he informed us that his girlfriend and her four-year-old daughter were coming over and we would all go out to eat. He met her in a singles group at his church. He also informed us that she was pregnant with his child and they would be getting married.

"Shocked" is an understatement. In the getting to know her phase, before going to the restaurant, we were forced with information faster than we could comprehend. The jumbled pieces of information were calling for questions we could not ask. Our future daughter-in-law told us she was divorced. By the time we got to the restaurant, we were emotionally and mentally wasted. There was no cohesion in all we heard. Spiritually, we had an awareness that we were no longer in our comfort zone. We were challenged and entering a new phase of growth.

Very little can be remembered about the remainder of the evening. Our future daughter-in-law, while attending the singles group at a Baptist church, was not a member of the church. Her family was of the Acadian or Cajun heritage from the Iberia Parish, south Louisiana tradition. The maternal grandparents were from Puerto Rico. Catholic churches dominated the area and children went to Catholic schools. We went back to the house and informed them that we would just head on back. We requested they seek counseling from the pastor and to keep us informed about the wedding plans. The little girl was hugging our legs as we left.

We drove about a hundred miles before stopping for the night. We were in considerable shock and disbelief. While riding, we were verifying and comparing what each of us thought we had heard and observed. Our son was in an obvious state of overwhelm and we hurt for his discomfort level. When we got home we called and made an appointment to meet with our pastor. Our pastor advised us to hire a private detective to clarify the baffling information about our future daughter-in-law's background. Mike had previously met one of the pastor's in the church our son attended and called him. He agreed it should be done and gave us a name to call.

In the meantime, we were getting no information from our son about wedding plans. The information from the detective verified everything we had wondered about and more. We tried to discuss with our son who was not surprised, but silent. The wedding date was set very soon after the encounter. Our future daughter-in-law started calling my mother and sister telling them how we hated her. She was most definitely on mission to destroy us and all of our family relations. She even convinced them that they needed to protect her from Shane's parents.

This was just what my Mom needed to start beating me again, not physically, but with emotional ramifications far greater than the physical beatings in days gone by. Other family members jumped in on the band wagon supporting all of the lies and untruths told to Mom. For years, even when we gave proof that we were not present on the dates of the alleged events, my family turned on us. It just did not matter that we were out of state, hundreds of miles away with friends. Our son became voiceless and our daughter-in-law controlled my family of origin. My mother rose to the occasion of "protecting" our son, her grandson, from his Mom and Dad.

When our grandson was born we were allowed to come see him. The infant was placed in Mike's hands for about two minutes as the mother stood over him, and then I got to hold him for a minute and then we were thanked for coming and dismissed. It was a shock to drive over 600 miles for less than a ten-minute visit. And that was the way that story went for years.

We did have another brief visit several months later. On arrival, there were household goods that Shane had taken from our home to Louisiana on his initial move, waiting on the carport for us to load into our car and bring back to South Carolina. The little girl, our step-granddaughter, wanted to show us her room. We were shocked to see sixty to seventy dolls all over the room. Special shelving was required to display all of the dolls. Our grandson was several months old and all seemed well with him.

We walked around in the yard and were surprised to see what we would call ant hills all over the yard. Then I realized they did not look exactly like the ant hills in South Carolina. I walked over to one and kicked at the soil and started uncovering body parts of a doll. Then I went around and every one of the dirt mounds I kicked had doll parts and some of them were burned. I quietly called Mike's attention to this. I did ask our son and he denied knowing anything about it. We stayed a few more hours and then left. Here again our trip home was consumed with shock and disbelief. When we got home, my Mom was calling wanting to know why we had been so mean to our daughter-in-law. There was no use in trying to explain that we had not spent the night with them and were not present at the time of an alleged event.

Mike's family was reality bound and had no appreciation for anyone that would treat us that way. Our Anderson family and church friends reached out to us at holidays in special ways since we no longer had contact with our son and my family. I appreciated the outreach from others but it did little to relieve the feeling of living in a deeply dug rock tomb. Our many visions and dreams for the future seemed out of reach.

In the meantime, I had continued my educational pursuits and was now in a doctoral program at the University of South Carolina while teaching nursing part-time at Clemson. Mike was working for an educational institution and had most of the summer off. My educational pursuits required some travel in the summers to places we had only heard about and never thought we could afford to visit. We enjoyed the travel but were never without that feeling of the hole in the soul.

The following year we had another grandchild born, a girl. She was about three months old before we were allowed to visit her. Once again, they had done their token duty and permitted us to visit. Holidays would come and go. We would send gifts but never received a response. However, our son and daughter-in-law were in constant touch with my larger family. They would even come to visit my family in South Carolina but never stop to see us. Triangulation seemed to be their master plan.

Eventually, when our granddaughter was two years old, Shane accepted a position in the upstate and they relocated to South Carolina. He did tell us he wanted to get back to his South Carolina roots for the sake of his children. They moved into a house we purchased for rental. We did get to see them occasionally but all was strained. However, it was better than not knowing where they were.

It was with good intention we had worked hard over the years to create a stable family environment for our son. Mike was gracious in accepting the differences in his family and mine. We did put much expectation on my family about coming for holiday meals. We were aware that we often had many pink elephants in the room but we had gotten used to what to expect. After 1993, we never had another family or holiday gathering in our home while both of my parents were alive. It did seem like all was lost. Sometimes I would find myself even missing the pink elephants.

Since my research focus in the doctoral studies was about family systems, I realized I was caught up in family dysfunction from another world. There was my history with my mother. I was most likely drawn to family systems research because of all of the unresolved issues in my own family of origin. I know I was highly motivated to create a stable home environment for our son that would reap happy days of grandparenting. I had lost my grandparents in late childhood and had always been envious of friends who grew up in relationship with their grandparents. Mike's grandparents had been around in the early years of our marriage and it filled a gap in my life. We had built a home in expectation of making many wholesome memories.

Reality was in front of me. I was forced to accept that all I had treasured and worked for was gone. Saying good-bye to a hoped-for life was a painful process. All that I went through with my mother in childhood was like playing in a sandbox compared to this. However, getting to the full realization that I was at the bottom of the tomb was the beginning of exploring my options for a new way of life and living. I had to find a way to live with the unacceptable.

I read self-help books and journaled. I also changed my Bible reading plan to a praying through the Bible plan and journaled those prayers, verse by verse. I prayed and journaled through several different versions of the Bible. And yes, it was much more than a thirty-minute devotional time each day. The journaling was healing for me. At times when the sorrow was carrying me deeper into the tomb, I could not pray. However, there was strength in going to the journals and reading prayers previously written. (Pieces and parts of the journaling journey are included in Appendix B).

I had noticed in my work with students in nursing homes, the residents often misplaced their Bibles. Some had limitations with hand use and could no longer pick up their Bible. From my prayer journals, I started making half page pamphlets with four pages containing prayers in large print and taking them to the nursing homes. The large print pamphlets were collections of prayers about hope or trust. They were always received well, easy to pick up and easy to re-place. My husband also found use for the prayer booklets on his job as he and a colleague led a weekly Bible study at his place of employment.

I can look back on it all now and say that in the direst of circumstances, we can trust our God to provide both the internal and external environments that will enable His children to thrive. Externally there were two major pathways created for me by my Lord and Savior. One of the external pathways also created the internal journey to health, healing, and wholeness.

The first of the external pathways provided to me was my academic journey. Within my focus on family systems, I targeted family resiliency for my concept of interest. The Institute of Families and Society had sponsored my research and offered me a position upon completion of the Ph.D. However, I declined and accepted a full-time teaching position at Clemson. With the position was an expectation that I would give presentations at conferences about my area of specialty. Therefore, I was constantly staying current with what the academic world thought about family dysfunction and the resilient approach for survival. Mike enjoyed learning about it and we both adopted some survival techniques.

At times I felt like I was making some progress in exiting the tomb of powerlessness. Then I would find myself on rock bottom again. The second external pathway the Lord provided me came by way of a job offer from the St. Francis Health System. This was totally unexpected. I resisted at first because I was well bolstered when thinking of being on track to become a fully tenured Clemson professor someday. I felt like my grandchildren may not know me now but someday it may mean something to them that their grandmother had been a Clemson professor. When I declined the position, I was asked by Sister Marilyn Trowbridge to enter into a season of prayer with them to reconsider the offer.

I asked Sister Marilyn why they would want a protestant to direct one of their community ministries. She explained that they needed a non-Catholic to carry the concept of health ministry to the protestant churches. She had attended some of my workshop series on family resiliency and related she knew we had similar values.

I would get regular phone calls asking if I had discerned. Then the day came when I did discern and accepted the position to start at the end of the semester. The position was directing the parish nursing ministries. There were conditions of special training I would have to participate in to strengthen me spiritually to represent the health system the way they desired. The position required me to facilitate nurses in the community who felt the Lord was calling them to work with those in their congregation with various needs related to health and healing.

The underlying assumption is that one must first be in touch with their own brokenness before they can genuinely assist another. Therefore, Sister Marilyn enrolled me in numerous retreats on health, healing, and wholeness. I was also provided a library of books to absorb. To insure my progress, I was enrolled in a program that required me to spend every Monday for a year at a nearby psychiatric hospital serving as a chaplain trainee along with six others.

I worked every Monday with the chaplains and we closed out the day with an hour of groupwork as we listened and critiqued each other's work of the day. We would relate the stories as told to us by our patients and then discuss ways to offer spiritual support, after assessing the point of greatest need. I was the only participant who was not a seminary student or ordained minister. Just think about it! I was getting paid to find my way up out of the tomb that had imprisoned me for several years.

I will always wonder if my toxicity cried out to the Franciscan Sisters of the Poor in Greenville. They had identified my skillset as one to contribute to the program development and educational offering they wanted to make available. Could they have also seen my brokenness and knew they could contribute to the pathway for my healing?

There was no mistaking that God had a plan for this suffering soul. My reality persisted around me, however, little by little the lightbulbs started coming on. The light of the goodness of God was opening a way for me.

CHAPTER SEVENTEEN

THE JOURNEY BEGINS

I THINK THE CHAPLAINS I worked with on Mondays took me on as one of their projects. To them, I was probably a flashing neon sign blinking things like: "Look at me. See what I have accomplished," "I didn't let my mother get the best of me," "I may have been raised on a mill village but I got an education," and "I go to church every time the doors are open." The chaplains were there with me as I realized my tomb was much deeper than the recent years of anguish. The journey to an utter, radical dependence on the Triune God of the universe had begun. It was not about me and how hard I could work and fix things. Trying to fix the broken things and act like everything was normal had become toxic.

There was no mistaking that I was grounded in a Christian world-view. I was expected to develop training programs for certified continuing education credits for nurses in general, but also to include specific content about the ministry of health, healing, and wholeness. The Biblical concepts embedded in the topics are unending. However, I was attending specific training events preneed about the desired content for the upcoming programs requiring development.

Every program I had to create carried me deeper in my faith walk. The weekly work with the chaplains kept drilling down to the core of my being.

A few months after all of this started, I was in one of the Monday chaplain group meetings and a discussion arose about the difference between guilt and shame. The leader asked us to close our eyes and think back to a time we experienced shame. He explained that shame was not about something you have done but about something done to you by another. My mind went back to that summer between the sixth and seventh grade when a shoe salesman would not try a pair of shoes on my bare feet because my feet were too dirty. I began to sob. The group was most supportive. Then the chaplain who was the supervisor of the group raised a question about why was I, at that young age, having to go alone to shop for school shoes. It was the beginning of the healing of my childhood wounds. I was in the right support group on a regular basis to do the necessary processing of all that had happened to me. All of my hard work and tenacity was just that. It had nothing to do with the healing of my emotional scars.

I had been made ready for this part of my journey. I was drawn closer to the Lord when my dream for wholesome family life started to unravel. My journey with the contemplative writers, and the journaling of my prayers and events had set forth a track for my life and living. Much of my daily time was dedicated to study.

As I trekked the pathway from the pure white cotton fields of innocence, through the downward, inward, and backward deep dark recesses of my reality, I learned the true meaning of contemplative silence. I began to understand that my healing was related to my silence with God. It was during these times of silence that God was very vocal, vocal with His Balm of Gilead making this wounded soul whole. I was blessed with discovery of contemplative silence. Slowly, I began to look forward to contemplating the noisy healing silence of God.

I came to understand the ruination of noise, and how noise leads the way for us to forsake our God of silence. The leading is both subtle and difficult to detect. The noise includes our wounds, and the turmoil, unrest, and agitation that accompany the wounds. No matter how hard we work to hide the wounds, the noise is present. The racket accomplishes one sinister goal, to rob us of our solitude. Without solitude, there is no meditative silence for the journey. This healing journey is a choice and must become a daily intentional act of our will. We cannot give power to the noise.

I was fifty-three years old and beginning to learn about my emotional and spiritual wounds. I was busy with my job requirements. The job carried me to a series of conferences that continued to enlighten me about spiritual wholeness. Learning about spirituality sufficient to teach about it took much study on my part. Reflection on my daily Bible reading and the contemplative writers continued as the mainstay. It was good to have the Monday group of chaplains for reflection. I needed to learn how to explain the meaning and purpose of life in plain language. The concepts had to be incorporated into the workshops I was required to develop. One's spirituality is evidenced in their purpose for living. The faith, healing, and prayer connection was making an entrance into the health care political arena to the degree that even the non-faith based health systems had to take heed. My job was to hold to the Christian worldview while the non-faith based health systems led with an interfaith position.

I must have been doing okay because I started getting invitations to speak at conferences and share the approach we were taking where I was employed. The topic was always about "The Integration of Faith and Health." It was challenging to develop training materials on the content holding to the Christian worldview while not offending those with opposing worldviews. My projected audiences were nurses from seventeen local denominations. On the red-eye flight back from such a meeting in San Diego, I was kept awake making notes on all I had learned at the meeting. I was enmeshing it with all of the study I was doing on the topic and the current level of my program development.

A few days after getting back to my routine, I received a call from Austin Theological Seminary in Austin, Texas. The caller was the editor of a quarterly journal published by the seminary. My name had been given to them by a mutual chaplain friend. The editor was preparing a journal issue focusing on healing and wholeness. They were seeking representatives from various disciplines to respond to a position paper on the topic. I agreed to consider a response. After reading their position paper, I accepted the opportunity to have my response published with the paper.[5]

Most of my response had already been written on the flight home from San Diego. I was shocked. It was not me but the Lord writing that paper on the plane in the middle of the night. It took about two days of refinements and verification of sources. Learning that my meaning and purpose on this earth comes from answering the call

---

5 Smith, Sybil. 1999. "Nursing in Churches, Response to God's Life Giving Ways." *Insights: The Faculty Journal of Austin Seminary*, Spring 1999 edition. Vol. 114.2, 29-32 http://www.austinseminary.edu/uploaded/about_us/pdf/insights/insights_1999_spring.pdf.

to become a steward of the faith changed my life forever. Folk are forever searching for meaning and purpose until they accept the call to become a steward of the faith. A person cannot become a genuine steward or agent of anything until its value is real. And now, placing that awakening into printed words for others to view had an impact I did not see coming. It was the legitimization of the healing process for me. It was the practical application of all of the head knowledge I had gained on my journey to wholeness. It also placed the content into plain language that was suitable for the lay audiences I was expected to teach (See Appendix C).

I do not want to give the wrong impression. There is no quick fix for soul pain. All of the things I have described took place over months and years. However, I did have the hope and faith to persevere. It had been implanted in me as a child living on the mill village.

My eyes became opened to those who suffered in silence, the forgotten all around us every day. One group I challenged the congregational nurses to work with was those with heavy grief burdens related to non-death losses. Special programs and materials were developed for guiding nurses to assist congregational lay people with such issues. I promoted a focus on aging parents who still had a prodigal, just wanting to see them one more time. Grant monies were obtained for contracting with grief and loss experts to refine the development of materials.

All of the baggage I carried was still with me but no longer in front of me. I walked with it every day but it was now beside me, not in the front. I found peace with my life and living, and was blessed to share it with others. My new guiding principles were not absent in my Baptist life, but were never taught in such a way that I could grab hold to the depth of my brokenness. I had a deep cup of sorrow to drink and God placed me in a wagon track which led me to become a steward of my faith. Drinking the cup of sorrow requires more than answering one alter call.[6]

As time moved on, we started having some contact with our son, his family, and my parents and siblings. There were no more gatherings at our home, even though we would extend the invitations. When they would decline, we would ask if we could come for a visit. When permitted, awkward does not begin to describe the visits. Our attempted phone calls, if answered, were brief. Years later we found out about some serious emergency health issues they had experienced and we had never been informed.

I started reading everything I could find on forgiveness issues. I had come through my grief and loss work. However, the grief and loss work was not the whole package. Tied up, and hiding in that package was the forgiveness issue that remained with my Mom. I read many books about forgiveness and attended a ladies Bible study with a focus on forgiveness. I could keep the forgiveness issues parked on the side of me except around holidays. I was aware of being left out on the holidays because I could not share the holidays with my parents, our son, and grandchildren. At one level I had let it all go, but sometimes during the holiday seasons my mind would wander to all that I was missing out on because of my Mom, sister, sister-in-law, and daughter-in-law. The four of them led a massive campaign, on several fronts, against us.

I thought the alienation was part of the loss and should be on the side of me along with the shock and awe of all that had happened

---

6 Henri J.M. Nouwen, *Can You Drink the Cup?* (Indiana: Ave Maria Press, 1996).

over my lifetime. I had learned to get up every day and thank God for what He was going to bring across my path that day. I learned to accept that what He brought to me was His plan for me. If my family was not a part of that day, it was acceptable since He knew what I needed. My focus was not on my losses but on my service to Him for that day. Surprisingly, there were many folk just like us with absent family during the holidays. A new type of family developed.

Our pastor gave us some good advice on how to deal with the special occasions. He referred to it as respect and duty care, since he was familiar with the depth of our loss. He felt we had come a long way in accepting our loss. The advice was to always send cards to the family members for special occasions to let them know we still remembered them. Our duty was to attend, in love, any event they did invite us to attend. Our love was to always be open to them and opportunities that may develop.

Finally, I made it to the right Bible study. It included a unit on feelings one might experience when they think they have worked through forgiveness issues, and yet, occasionally sense some uncomfortableness. One of the learning exercises asked us to think about someone with whom we may have felt we had forgiven but yet some fallout remains. My thoughts went to my Mom and no one else. The writer asked us to consider if there were at least two things about the person, no matter how we had been wronged, for which we could thank God. On reflection, I found three things for which I could thank my Mom. First, she had given me life and brought me into this world. From her life in the Baptist orphanage, she knew she needed to keep her family in church. One could say she gave me a compass for my life. Then the facts that she had taught me to cook and to sew came to light.

Being able to cook and sew were life-savers for the early years of our marriage. Indeed, I had developed those skills at the hands of my Mom. The exercise further challenged us to make a daily practice of thanking God for those gifts. From that point to this day of writing I always, in my morning prayer, thank God for my Mom giving me life, taking me to church, and that she taught me to cook and sew. Time passed. Holidays came and went and I never experienced alienation again. The Bible study further helped me to drill down in understanding solidarity with Christ. There is no pain and suffering in solidarity. Solidarity is peace. It is available to me every day. The past does not change. Full forgiveness does allow me to go forward in love, thanking God each day for His goodness as it will unfold for me each day. In solidarity, there is no entombment.

My life was immersed in my spiritual walk and I did not realize the ramifications of what was happening in my professional work. I had an unexpected phone call from a famous physician researcher in the field of faith and health at Duke University. The call came in a few weeks after the September 11, 2001 event. He was aware of my work with nurses involved in congregational ministries. I was asked to write a book collecting the local stories of the parish nurses involved in the pioneering days of health ministry. It took some time to think through how I could deliver on such a project, but I finally decided to sign a contract and accepted a cash advance. The book was published in 2003 entitled: *Parish Nursing: A Handbook for the New Millennium*. Shortly after the book came out, I was asked to serve on a committee to develop the Scope and Standards of Practice for Faith

Community Nursing for the American Nurses Association, which was published in 2005.

The recognition was but a blip on my radar. My professional colleagues employed by the universities were envious. I was not concerned with the next line on my curriculum vitae. Time was passing and new family situations started developing all around us that had the possibility of placing demands on us. We became focused on our readiness to be available as needed.

CHAPTER EIGHTEEN

FINDING MY LOST TREASURES

MY PARENTS WERE ENTERING THE ninth decade of their life by the mid-2000s. Their health status remained stable but age appropriate. They did become open to our visits. My Mom started showing signs of forgetfulness and confusion and became dramatic when you tried to suggest reality. My Dad continued to work part-time for my brother's accounting firm. Dad would deliver payroll to a few small businesses that did not want to modernize to computers. Dad was the coffee break special when he made deliveries.

Mom had quit going to church a few years earlier. Dad still enjoyed his church fellowship and visitation with the homebound. Driving was no longer an option for Mom because she could never find her way home. When we would visit with them, I would take Mom to shop or out for a ride. She never knew where she was and was constantly demanding I turn when she said to turn because I did not know the way home. The day she tried, from the passenger seat, to take control of the steering wheel away from me, was my last day to carry her for an outing. I found out later that she had been doing the same thing with Dad. However, she had convinced my brother and sister that it was Dad that would get lost and not her. I think Dad, just wearied from the struggle with her, and no longer wanted to drive with her in the car.

Mike and I made a conscious decision to back out of our weekly Sunday church obligations and become available to go to Rock Hill every other Sunday and take Dad to church. It was a real joy to observe my Dad interact with his friends. Often, Dad would also ask Mike to take him to visit some of his homebound friends. When I was a child and we lived on the Harris Mill Village, my Dad always visited the homebound and the weekly absentees from church. And here he was now in his mid-eighties, continuing to visit the homebound.

During this time, we did have occasional contact with our son and his family, not because we did not desire more. We learned to be thankful for what was available to us. Our son's work had transferred him to the midlands of the state. Whenever he had to come back to the upstate for a meeting, Shane would call and we would meet up for a cup of coffee. The times were brief but the updates on the kids were good.

Mike and I had become facilitators for The Truth Project when it was originally launched by the Focus on the Family Ministry. We led the thirteen-week study in the Spring and Fall each year. We had just completed a Spring session prior to one of the meet ups with Shane and as we shared what we had been doing, a spark of interest was observed. I realized we had never carried the tote bag with the teaching materials into the house after the last session. The DVDs were in the trunk of our car. When offered, Shane accepted the opportunity to take the set of DVDs home for personal study. And that was a new beginning for him.

Our son called a few days later and with sounds of sniffling on the phone, he thanked us for the DVDs. He further related that he had been taken back to the God of his childhood and wanted to talk more with us about it all. Indeed, God answers prayers! Our son had been able to keep his children in church as his wife was mostly an observer. As the days moved on, we could see that our son was commencing his own healing journey. Several books could be written about the healing journeys in his life and the lives of our grandchildren. In the depths of much aching reality, the grandchildren were nurtured by youth pastors and church family and made it to college.

In the meantime, our visits with my parents were taking a new dimension. Even as Mom's condition was changing, she could still bake a delicious ol' time Southern biscuit. Mike decided this was a tradition that must be passed on. Since I had no interest in biscuit making, Mike was determined to learn. He spent a couple of weekends in Rock Hill, and he and Mom baked batch after batch of biscuits. Mike did ask her to write down the recipe. The struggle for her to get the recipe written shows up on the document. After about the third batch on the third weekend, and with no assistance from his teacher, Mom announced that Mike had a perfect batch. After the kitchen was cleaned that day, Mom gathered all of her biscuit making utensils, along with her hand-written copy of the recipe and passed it in an official, dramatic way over to Mike. She never baked biscuits again, but did expect Mike to bring her some biscuits on every visit.

As I have thought back on all that went into the weekends of biscuit making, for Mom, it must have been seen as passing on part of her heritage from the orphanage. A few years later, she asked Mike to teach our granddaughter how to make the biscuits. It was April of 2010 when Mike did teach our granddaughter how to make the biscuits and passed on to our granddaughter the utensils and recipe learned by her great-grandmother while growing up in the orphanage.

Even though I was a nurse specialized in the care of older persons, my brother and his wife decided, with no input from me, to move Mom and Dad out to their house in a rural farming area. The scenery was beautiful with a stream and pond with various ducks coming in and out. The farm across the highway had unusual farm animals to observe. There was a llama, unusual goats, a few donkeys, chicken and sheep. The scenery made sitting on the front porch and waving to passersby a pleasant pass time. Down the road from my brother's property was large acreage that turned into beautiful white cotton fields during the late summers.

On our trips back and forth to rural York County, we were able to observe the cotton fields from freshly planted, to the yellow blooms, and in the fall, the full white cotton boll. The harvesting process was much different from anything I had remembered from childhood. When we carried Dad out for a ride, he enjoyed seeing the cotton. Sometimes we would stop and take pictures standing in the field as we pondered the memories. Where would our life be, had it not been for the cotton. Indeed, beneficial life lessons had been learned from our cotton mill heritage.

By this time, my Mom refused to speak of anything from the past. She became very critical of anyone who wanted to remember the past. Even though she was frequently confused about time and place, she became very dogmatic about not recalling the past. Everybody learned not to ask about the past. She was also dogmatic about not going to doctors. When she started falling and breaking bones, she was most non-compliant about all care instructions and follow through. Eventually, my brother did place both Mom and Dad in an assisted living facility.

Mom's condition continued to deteriorate. It became apparent that her care needs were beyond the scope of assisted living. My brother paid care managers to tell him what he wanted to hear. With my background I could see how the situation was going to play out down the road. Mike and I became proactive in advocating for Dad to be placed in the nursing home for veterans in Anderson. After all, Dad would be among veteran friends he went to church with while living in Anderson. Several from Orrville Baptist Church were now residents in the facility.

In reality, we wanted to bring Dad to our home but knew my brother was not ready to let go of that much control. As Mom's condition repeated the cycle of hospitalization and back to facility, over and over, my brother did begin the process of exploring the Veteran's facility for Dad. We convinced him of our near proximity to the facility and that we could make his load lighter as he managed Mom's care.

It happened! We were able to get Dad relocated to the Richard Campbell VA facility in Anderson, South Carolina. It was a substantial upgrade from where he had been staying. The nursing staff was plentiful and well trained in needs of older and infirmed persons. All residents received active physical therapy every week. I was surprised to see such a large number of physical therapists on staff. Activities abounded, which were provided internally and also from the community. Family events were scheduled weekly. It was made easy for us to come and have a meal with Dad. We visited four to five times per week as did most of the families.

After a few weeks, when we had shared our story with others about Dad's military service and his hometown, we suddenly became aware of five other families in the facility from Greenwood. They were hearing about us and we all finally did get caught up with one another. Surprisingly, three of the residents were from the same neighborhood where my Dad grew up, the Greenwood Mill Village. They all knew each other as kids and went to the same school. My Dad had even taught one of the men how to play baseball. The family members were familiar with my Dad's textile league baseball success. However, they all went off to war, World War II, when they got out of high school.

The dining room was always full of residents and their families. There was a sense of all being one big family. We shared the meal in a common dining room. We shared the same walking trails as we carried our loved ones on outdoor strolls. We assisted one another with rolling chair issues because some of the veterans required more complex style of rolling chair than others. Some family members were too fragile themselves to manage certain maneuvers. There were many blessings from the church groups that would come in and sing. We got to know, not only the other veterans, but their families in a genuine way. We learned each other's visitation schedule and would check in on one another's loved one when the family was not present.

In warm weather, the holiday events were held in a large picnic shelter area with live music and delicious food for all. The Sunday lunch was always a big family event in the dining room of the facility.

The unity of the spirit among the families was unexpected and powerful. I started feeling it as similar to what I had experienced as a child when living on the Harris Mill Village. There was intense unity in the community of the veterans and their families. How could it be? The facility was not a church. It was constantly on my mind. The only rational thought I could conjure was since all of the veterans had been on a common mission in war, we indeed shared a common vision and hoped-for-life. The unity of the community was real and most satisfying. You could sense it in the demeanor of the veterans. As we would push Dad down a corridor, it was common for the men to salute one another if they had use of their arms. Every visit was a major uplift for us. I believed it to be a spiritual experience.

There was an unspoken bond among the families. The connection also existed among the veterans in various ways of expression, dependent on physical limitations. For some it was the salutes. For others, it could be a pat on the hand, a nod, the glow in the eyes, and for those who could speak, it was praise and gratitude. We were surrounded by much brokenness. Not only were there the deteriorating conditions of the veterans, but there was heaviness of heart of the family members as they lived their reality each day. The yielding of expectations every day drew forth an abounding wholeness, producing unity in community.

The experience was much like Michael Card's song, "The Basin and the Towel" (See Appendix A). There were powerful relationships of caring for one another among the veterans and their families. Some days we would be carrying the basin and the towel, and would kneel in service to another. On other days, we might be the one with our feet in the basin. Indeed, the call to community was valued.

In the meantime, back in Rock Hill, my Mom's condition was getting worse. She quickly went from being wheelchair bound to bedbound. We would go to see her on Wednesdays. She had come to accept her dependence on others. We would always take her a new picture of Dad and vice versa. When able, I attended a morning Bible study at my church before going to Rock Hill. The study started one morning with a song by Michael Joncas, "We Come to Your Feast" (See Appendix D). I became emotional with every mention of the work of our hands.

On our previous visit to see Mom, I had carried her a memory board. It was a large trifold poster board where I had placed pictures of some of her sewing projects and crafts over the years. When I gave Mom the board, she shed tears and thanked us, relating she still knew her name but had forgotten what she had done in her life. We also reminded her of her good cooking and the biscuits.

As soon as I left the Bible study, I stopped and bought some grape juice and bread. I was able to get the song up on my Kindle. I quickly located table linens made by Mom from fabric out of the cotton mill I had worked in as a nurse. I had been able to get several yards of the finished fabric and Mom had sewn table linens from the material and embroidered on them in the 1970s.

We loaded up and headed for Rock Hill. When we walked into her room, I could tell her days were short. She had some smiles and patted our hands and pointed to her memory board from the week earlier. Her voice was less than a whisper. We played the song, "We Come to Your Feast," on the Kindle as I spread the white linen table cloth, made by her hands, over the bedside table. We placed the bread and juice on the table. All three of us dipped our bread into the juice and placed it in our mouth. Mom had some slight trouble swallowing at first, and then a huge smile came across her face as some facial wrinkles seemed to thaw out. Mike prayed. She declared with excitement that we had taken communion. She smiled and patted our hands over and over, but uttered no more words. A few days later, she passed away. The work of her hands covered her casket with a quilt of many embroidered bluebirds.

With heavy hearts, we knew we were going to have to let Dad know about Mom. When we informed him, he became somber with tears in his eyes. The staff was sensitive to his needs as well as our new larger family of families. On an outside stroll with Dad as we walked the edge of the woods, he saw some birds and related how Mom had enjoyed birds. We started calling the birds Mattie birds. One day he corrected us, that she preferred red birds. We agreed that only the red birds were to be called Mattie birds.

Mike and I decided that we were going to start the process to get Dad moved to our home for the remainder of his time. My brother was the first step since he was named as power over everything. He did not understand our request but did agree that we could. There were many steps to work through but it all flowed. Some of our close friends thought we were nuts, saying we did not know what we were getting into. However, we prayed, counted the cost, and we knew exactly what we were getting into.

When we built our house in Lyman in the 1970s and did a walk through with Dad for the first time, we had laughed about the beautiful view from the triple windows in the den. It gazed across a large open field and a hillside beyond with cows grazing. We told him that when he got old, we would put his sick bed in front of the windows so he would have a peaceful view. We laughed back then, but now the day was here. It took a couple weeks to get everything ready. There was a ramp to be built, the rearrangement of furniture and turning our middle bedroom into a supply room. The VA made the paperwork easy. Dad was admitted to their palliative care homebound program. Nothing was overlooked. Doctors, social workers, nurses, and therapists all came to the house. All supplies were delivered in advance on a regular basis.

From his bed, Dad enjoyed watching the cars go up and down the road, the dogs playing in the field across from us, and describing the color of the vehicles he saw going up and down the road on the far side of the field. When up in his wheelchair, he always wanted to go onto the deck. From the deck, he expected to go down the ramp and out to the end of the driveway. He loved to watch the cars go by and waved at everyone. The neighbors got to know him in their own way and some of the kids would come by and sing with him.

The nutritionist from the VA came out to the house to make sure I was comfortable with pureeing Dad's food. She gave me the same advice Aunt Monte had given my mother years ago as she had cared for my grandmother in her closing days: only fix his favorite foods. She surmised he had loved tomato sandwiches and told me to put the ingredients into the blender with much mayonnaise. Even though it was puree, the smile on his face told you he remembered the taste fondly. We did the same thing with peanut butter and jelly sandwiches and peach cobbler.

My sister, who did not attend our mother's funeral, would come down to visit, as well as my brother and his wife. The condition I put on the visits was that they were all welcome, at all times, but they needed to bring the meal when they came. Dad would sit at the table in his wheelchair with his pureed food and enjoy the family fellowship as we ate whatever showed up. Our niece and nephew and their young families came as well as our son and grandchildren. Once again, we had frequent and wholesome family fellowship in our home. How long had it been? During football season, we had game watching parties and Dad would comment every time he saw a runner with the ball. On one occasion, Dad even told my brother not to talk so much. Our son was present every weekend and the grandkids, now in college, came as schedules permitted.

The ramp had made a way for Dad to have access to some good quality closing days to his life. For Mike and I, the ramp made our house a home again. We had regained volumes more than we had lost. We were together in reality.

On every visit from the doctor, he accepted the offer to sit down for coffee and cake and give an update of where Dad was in the closing of his earthly days. The next day the social worker would come out to make sure we understood it all. On one occasion, the social worker took care to inform us of Dad's specific job in the Army during World War II. She informed us he had been a spy. We knew he had been in Special Operations but never in those words. She wanted us to not be alarmed of some of the things he may speak about in those last hours.

The day came when the team suggested the time was now that we needed to transfer Dad from palliative care to hospice care. I was not surprised. After all, I am a nurse. The transition to the hospice team went well. Dad started talking during the night. He had conversations with my Mom and with his sister. One time he made a statement that made me wonder if it was military oriented. I started losing much sleep and developed a sore throat. All of this was going down during Thanksgiving Week. The hospice nurse suggested we consider a five-day hospice home admission to regulate his meds and for me to get an uninterrupted night of rest and get beyond the sore throat. A bed was expected to become available the next day and they were starting the paperwork process.

The next day was Thanksgiving and our son and grandkids were expected. Mike had to take over most of the meal fixing due to my sore throat. This was our grandson's year to carve the turkey. Everybody was made current on what was happening. Dad did not rise to a level of awareness that morning sufficient to try to get him into the wheelchair. He was taking very little liquid. At the time we were ready to sit down for Thanksgiving lunch, the phone rang. It was the hospice home and they were sending a transport to pick up Dad. We made a quick decision that I would follow the transport and they were to finish eating and then come to the hospice home. Our grandson got up immediately and went to Dad's bedside. He held his hand and prayed with him until the transport arrived.

The admission process could not have gone better. I had carried Dad's favorite music CDs. All I had to do was load a CD in the provided player and just sit there and listen with Dad. The staff took care of everything, including me. It wasn't long before the family started arriving and I was sent home to go to bed. Before I left the room, our son showed me a photo he snapped as Dad left the house and was being loaded into the transport. There were tears in Dad's eyes.

Mike was able to arrange for someone to sit with Dad by evening and came on home. We both slept all night for the first time in a long time. My throat started getting better. I did not go back to the hospice home as Mike went every day. My brother, sister, and spouses spent the day with Dad on Sunday. When it was time for Dad to return on Monday, I was in good shape.

After returning home on Monday, Dad never did get in the wheelchair again. He was taking less and less liquid and nutrition drink. We had personal care assistants who came to sit with Dad two shifts a day. His medications had been changed and made the expected contribution to his lethargy.

On Thursday, he had taken only about six ounces of liquid by late afternoon. The hospice chaplain came by the house and the four of us had communion. The loaf and juice was placed on Dad's lower lip as he responded with some lip movement. The chaplain, Mike, and I sang "Amazing Grace." The chaplain left and Mike went to run an errand. I turned on Dad's music. I hugged him, told him I loved him, thanked him for all he had done for me, and that I was sitting right by the bed holding his hand. He was so peaceful, with a smile and normal looking skin even though his breaths were shallow. Our son called and I told him what I was doing, that my Dad's breaths were shallow but the sheets were still moving.

While on the phone with our son, the sheets quit moving and I could feel no air exchange. Shane stayed with me on the phone as I was looking for our other phone to call the hospice number. When I looked toward the door, the sitter for the evening was coming in. She took over and called hospice. Shane refused to hang up until Mike returned home. I was not crying. I experienced a peaceful calm.

God had blessed me with being able to honor my Dad in his dying as Dad had honored me in my birth. In caring for my Dad, there was the restoration of my lost treasures. Restoration was

claimed via the journey to utter, radical dependence on the Triune
God of this universe.

EPILOGUE

HOPE: A JOURNEY OF DEPENDENCE

Rom. 5:1-5; Rom. 8:24-25; Eph. 1:18

May 28, 2001

God calls us to peace, well-being, restoration, reconciliation with Him, others, and salvation in its fullest sense. In grace, we can claim the peace and rejoice in the hope of our salvation.

The events of daily living can result in turbulence and become disruptive to our sense of well-being and peace. Maintaining an inner peace in the midst of our tribulations is learned by obedience.

Obedience is intentional and a journey of faith through stages of dependence. The journey of faith teaches dependence and culminates in the Hope that will never disappoint.

The first stage of dependence is one that surfaces as tribulations begin to encroach our comfort zone. When tribulations surface, we take a posture of dependence during the hard times which may not be the same posture we maintain when our circumstances are unchallenged. Often this stage of dependence is mixed with self, praying the words, "God, you are in control," while at the same time lending fleshly input to work out or manipulate through problems.

Dependence at this stage will yield some perseverance because we are willing to go the distance, but are decisively vested in the outcomes.

Through perseverance we become weary and drained because of the physical effort and coping strategies employed to bring about outcomes. As hard as we may persevere, the outcomes can disappoint us. Once we realize God alone is in charge of the outcomes, character is developing in the form of utter dependence. In utter dependence, we realize God does not need us to help run the universe.

In utter dependence, we develop character. From character, we learn a radical dependence. Radical dependence on the Triune God of relationship is learned when we yield all of our expectations to God and live in His Hope.

When we know the hope of radical dependence, we are never let down or disappointed by our circumstances or burdens we bear. We can bear our burdens in joy because we know the Hope in them.

APPENDIX A

INTRODUCTION

The Basin and the Towel
by Michael Card 1994
Used with permission

In an upstairs room, a parable is just about to come alive.
And while they bicker about who's best,
with a painful glance, He'll silently rise.
Their Savior Servant must show them how
through the will of the water
and the tenderness of the towel.

Chorus:
And the call is to community,
The impoverished power that sets the soul free.
In humility, to take the vow,
that day after day we must take up the basin and the towel.

In any ordinary place,
on any ordinary day,
the parable can live again

when one will kneel and one will yield.
Our Saviour Servant must show us how
through the will of the water
and the tenderness of the towel.

bridge:
And the space between ourselves sometimes
is more than the distance between the stars.
By the fragile bridge of the Servant's bow
we take up the basin and the towel.

(chorus)

APPENDIX B

CHAPTER 16

PRAYER JOURNAL ENTRIES

Thank you Lord that your Word is settled in heaven and your faithfulness endures to all generations. We can trust your Word to carry us through any and all affliction. We can trust you to hear our prayers, and in your faithfulness answer us in your righteousness. Surround us with your peace Lord, for where you are no ill can abound. We trust your covenant of peace, which cannot be removed, to shower us with blessings. Psalm 119:89-92; 143:1; Isaiah 54:10; Ezekiel 34:25-26; Micah 5:4-5

People are working against me God. I am being falsely accused. I am broken hearted. They are so cruel. God, I could not endure this without belief in your goodness. Even the psalmist has said "I would have fainted had I not believed." Psalm 27:13

Oh Lord, you are my strength. Psalm 28:7

There is joy on the other side of these tears. Psalm 30:5

Thank-you Father for staying near to this broken heart. Psalm 34:18

Dear God, I want to journey toward the wholeness you have for me. Sometimes it is a painful and difficult path. You have healing for my wounds. You can mend all of my active bleeds. Release me God from the bondage of bad and painful memories. May I forgive those who have hurt me. With forgiveness, I can be free to fully experience becoming a steward of the faith in Jesus' name. Amen

Thank-you God for giving me the grace to choose healing in the midst of my suffering. I can choose healing because your work is perfect. Your ways are just and your judgements are right.

Your Son has provided the gift of healing. Because I carry His death with me I have His Life. In His Life, I can learn through my afflictions, and my weaknesses are made perfect.

Because my life in faith on this earth does not exempt me from difficulties I claim your promise of preservation from the evil in them. I choose healing Heavenly Father from the troubles of this world, in Jesus' name. Amen.

Thank-you Lord for this day. Thank-you for what you will bring across my path today.

I can trust that what you bring across my path will be for your purposes today, and is preparation for tomorrow. Esther 4:14

Thank-you Lord for the strength of your might, and the power of your Spirit to hold on and never let go of your promises. Regardless of the weariness of the struggles, I know I am secure and can trust you to never abandon me. Job 1:22; 2:9

Thank-you, Lord, that I can trust you to make my way and to keep my way. No matter what happens I trust you to preserve me for I am attached to your truth. I become stronger every day when I live your truth within, and practice your truth without. The integrity you build will stand the test of time. Job 17:9; 6:29

Lord, I choose to establish my foundation in your truth— the rock that will never be shaken in time of difficulty. Give me Lord the integrity of Job that never lets go even when it seems all is lost. I will never lose hope for I trust your power to keep me. Luke 6:48; Job 6:29

Because my times are in your hands I can trust you to deliver me from my enemies. I can trust your face to shine upon me. I can trust your goodness which you prepared for me. I can trust you to strengthen my heart. I can trust you to provide this broken vessel with courage and hope. Because I trust you O God, I can know you will lay up goodness for me. Psalm 31:12-24

Lord, I acknowledge my sin to you. It cannot be hidden. My transgressions are before you. I can trust you Lord to forgive my sin. Psalm 25:7

Instruct me Lord. Teach me your way. Guide me with your eye. I do not want to be like the mule. Surround me with your mercy. Psalm 32:8-10

Thank-you Lord, that your angel camps out with those who trust you; that those who trust you lack for nothing. I can trust you Lord to hear my cry. I can trust you Lord to deliver me. I can trust you Lord to stay near. Psalm 34:7-18

Lord, I trust your life-giving ways. I trust your instruction. I trust you to deliver me from discomfort. I trust you to bring relief. I trust your mercy to hold me up. I trust your comfort for my soul for you are my God, the rock of refuge. Psalm 94:16-22

Forgive me Lord for complaining. May I accept your boundary each day for I want to live in your statutes. I can trust you Lord to carry me to Elim where there are twelve wells of your water for me. Exodus 15:26-27

Father I want to choose your plans for me each day. I have to forego my desires and submit to the boundaries you place around me. The cost of submitting to you may seem high, but is the path to peace in the end. Luke 14:27-28

Lord there are many things around me that could discourage me. Send O Lord enough Gospel Light for me to readily see and avoid anything that would take my eyes off you. Lord I want to keep focused on you in both my external living and also in my inner being. I do not want to deceive myself with secret entanglements. I want to surrender wholly to the boundaries you provide for me and stay the course in the race you have marked out. Hebrews 12:1; Hebrews 3:12-15

To you O Lord I give thanks for you are good to me. I trust your mercy for me. It will endure forever. I trust you Lord to hear the cries of this fool. I thank you Lord for sending your Word to me. It is your Word with its Divine power that defeats all enemies and brings health and healing to this broken heart. Thank you for your love which endures forever. Thank you for the boundaries you have set for me. Acts 17:26

Thank you Lord for the pain and suffering which have come across my life, for they have taught me utter, radical, dependence on you. Thank you for teaching me how to freely live in the boundaries you provide for me each day. Thank you for your forgiveness for all of the years I have lived trying to make my own way, thinking my wellbeing was dependent on me. Though I have lived out my consequences, my scars allow me to carry the healing you brought to me to others—the joy of living in radical dependence in the boundaries of this day! Hebrews 5:8

Thank you Lord for my provision for this day. It is with gratitude I accept today your boundaries and provision for me. And tomorrow, with your grace and mercy, I will discover my boundaries for tomorrow. James 4:13-15

Thank you Lord for my boundaries even if they mean living at the hands of oppressors. In your peace I can be patient until the coming of the Lord. Give me the perseverance of Job who found the end you intended for him, the end of great compassion and mercy. Thank you for the freedom that comes from living in your boundaries, the freedom for my yes to mean yes and my no to mean no. James 5:7-12

Father, thank you for your Spirit that I can trust today—to hover over—just as your spirit hovered over in the beginning of creation. Your spirit hovered over the incomplete processes until your creation was complete. Your spirit hovers over me and the ones I love today for we are in the process of becoming complete in you day by day. We can be complete this day only as we accept the boundaries you provide for this day. We praise your name for a day is coming when we can be perfectly complete in you. Thank you for your grace and mercy which hovers over. Genesis 1:2

Forgive me Lord when I complain about my circumstances. When I complain, I am shutting down the Light of your Glory, the Gospel Light. The Gospel Light is available to expose whether my difficult circumstances are a result of my own doing, my own poor judgment about my priorities. Lord I need your Gospel Light so I can carefully discern your truth in these circumstances and seek wise counsel. In the Light of your Glory I can accept the boundaries you place around me today. When I fail to accept the boundaries you provide for me I make matters worse and more stressful. Exodus 17:2-4

O Lord God on high, we know you are more mighty than all of the troubles that surround us today. Your Word teaches that sufferings do come to your children. May we see the suffering in our life today as our boundary for this day, and find our healing in accepting this boundary. For those who are suffering this day, and do not know you as the Great Physician, make us their connection to You O God, as we leave your sweet fragrance with every step we take. Psalm 91

Thank You, Lord, for setting my boundaries. I cannot go beyond the Word of God to do less or more on my own. Numbers 22:18; 24:13

Because I believe, I can see the unseen. Because I believe, I can behold what is not near. Numbers 24:17

Father I can trust Your boundary lines to fall in pleasant places. Psalm 16:6

Sometimes Lord a sense of miserableness comes over me. Lord it can be hard to think about going forward. I am cut off from my visions and dreams for a hoped for life on this earth. My cherished plans for growing old have been cut off. Lord I give all of these cherished visions and dreams to you and I submit to your plans and purposes for me. Let me cheerfully surrender to your boundaries for my life. Job 17:11

Thank you Lord for hearing my cry, for lifting me out of the slimy pit, out of the mud and mire. Thank you for setting my feet on a rock and giving me a place to stand. Thank you for placing a new song on my lips, as I lift my hands in praise! Thank you for providing my boundaries, assigning me my portion and cup. Because you make my heart secure, I can live with no fear of bad news, for I know that in the end I can look in triumph on my foes. Thank-you for your strength and blessing of peace in the midst of all circum- stances. Even though we have burdens to bear and must go through fire and water, you bring us to an abundance of peace. Psalm 40

Dear Heavenly Father, I claim your peace.
-The peace the Holy Spirit brought to me,
-The peace the Holy Spirit taught me about,
-The peace the Holy Spirit causes me to remember when I feel anxious.

I am not afraid because you have taught me to live within the boundaries you provide for each day. I am not afraid because I surrender to the boundaries you provide. I want each step I take to be where you have already placed your feet before me. Give me sure footing as I journey this path. Lord I pray for a lifestyle of spontaneous obedience. Thank you Lord for allowing me to claim your peace. John 14:15-31; 16:12-13; Psalm 18:36

APPENDIX C

CHAPTER 17

PLAIN LANGUAGE PARAGRAPH

The integration of faith and health is about becoming equipped with a capacity to endure the onslaughts of life—the spiritual, emotional, behavioral, and psychological ups and downs. Enduring the onslaughts of life is learned in the techniques of suffering, otherwise known as living the life of biblical discipleship. Biblical discipleship is learned in the formation of faith as we respond to the call to become a child of God, our salvation. Secondly, after becoming a child of God we must respond to the call to become a disciple of God and to make Him Lord of our life. Real meaning and purpose come when we respond to a third call, to become a steward of the faith. When we miss the first call we live in lost-ness. Missing the second call plays out as we endure the consequences of bad decisions. When we do not become a steward of the faith, we will always be searching for meaning and purpose. Suffering is felt in many forms when we live without meaning and purpose. Our purpose for living must be big enough to prepare us for dying (Phil. 1:21).

First published in *Insights: The Faculty Journal of Austin Seminary,* Spring 1999 edition. Vol. 114.2 and is reprinted with permission.

http://www.austinseminary.edu/uploaded/about_us/pdf/insights/insights_1999_spring.pdf.

APPENDIX D

CHAPTER 18

WE COME TO YOUR FEAST

Verse 1

We place upon your table
a gleaming cloth of white:
the weaving of our stories,
the fabric of our lives;
the dreams of those before us,
the ancient hopeful cries,
the promise of our future:
our needing and our nurture
lie here before our eyes.

REFRAIN
We come to your feast,
we come to your feast:
the young and the old,
the frightened, the bold,
the greatest and the least.

We come to your feast,
we come to your feast
with the fruit of our lands
and the work of our hands,
we come to your feast.

Verse 2

We place upon your table
a humble loaf of bread:
the gift of field and hillside,
the grain by which we're fed;
we come to taste the presence
of him on whom we feed,
to strengthen and connect us,
to challenge and correct us,
to love in word and deed.

REFRAIN

Verse 3

We place upon your table
a simple cup of wine:
the fruit of human labor,
the gift of sun and vine;
we come taste the presence
of him we claim as Lord,
his dying and his living,
his leading and his giving,
his love in cup outpoured.

REFRAIN

Verse 4

We gather 'round your table,
we pause within our quest,
we stand beside our neighbors,
we name the stranger "guest."
The feast is spread before us;
you bid us come and dine:
in blessing we'll uncover,
in sharing we'll discover
your substance and your sign.

REFRAIN

Text and Music by Michael Joncas

For more information about

Sybil Smith
and

Thank God for the Cotton
please visit:

www.tgforthec.com
info@tgforthec.com
@TGfortheC
www.facebook.com/
Thank-God-for-the-Cotton-161882461037270

For more information about
AMBASSADOR INTERNATIONAL
please visit:

www.ambassador-international.com
@AmbassadorIntl
www.facebook.com/AmbassadorIntl

If you enjoyed this book, please consider leaving us a review on
Amazon, Goodreads, or our website.